AF588522

Journey of Crimson Threads

Beatrice Ostlie

Copyrights

Visit our website at www.nimbusublishers.com

First Edition: May, 2024

Book Published by Mr. Chris Walker & Joe Thompson on behalf of Nimbus Publishers.

For Don, Nichole, and Kimberly, my precious jewels.

The brilliance that shines from each of you Brings clarity to my journey of purpose.

Contents

Introduction 1

Chapter 1 Wednesday's Child 4

Chapter 2 Estelle 14

Chapter 3 All is Lost 22

Chapter 4 The Oldest Profession 32

Chapter 5 Adoption 42

Chapter 6 Bondage 52

Chapter 7 Fight-or-flight 62

Chapter 8 Awakening 72

Chapter 9 Reenter Estelle 80

Chapter 10 Dark Secrets Revealed 88

Chapter 11 Andy 98

Chapter 12 Breaking Free 104

Introduction

Harry Holt once said, "Our creator knows you intimately, even to the number of hairs on your head. He holds you in the palm of his hand. You are meant to be in existence. You are not an accidental happening." These positive words became an intricate thread of strength weaving through my DNA. Those words have echoed throughout my life to this day, tempering the icy cold of life's winters each time my emotionally frostbitten inner self has reached its comforting warmth.

His words crashed through storm-cresting waves that threatened to drown me in an ocean of despair and fear, offering me a life ring of positivity, thrusting me to the surface to see the lighthouse on the rocky cliffs above me—its beam guiding me toward calm, solid ground.

Writing this book has brought clear and precise confirmation of those words spoken so long ago. As an abandoned child, I had to build my arsenal of emotional strength. Only later did I realize that Harry's encouraging words were being internalized in a safe place—unconsciously hoarded until I was old enough and strong enough to forge them into an armament of courage. After I had struggled through years of degradation and claims that I had no right to my existence on this earth, Harry's words blazed forth, and I was propelled toward that lighthouse, its beams piercing the fog of circumstance to guide me.

The definition of a witness is one who has experienced an event or happening. If the thing witnessed is something terrible, a witness will feel shock or sadness, tragedy, trauma, or loss. Part of the price exacted by surviving the experience is the license, understanding, and desire to reach out to others. I hope that sharing Beatrice's story—my story—will help someone find healing and their own path to personal validation and self-worth.

Some details have been left out, and some names have changed for reasons that will, I trust, become clear

Chapter 1
Wednesday's Child

Bea's tiny feet were constantly sucked into a muddy swamp of fear that gripped her tiny appendages with every step forward from one day to the next. Upon hearing a poem in the first few years of her adoption—a bouquet of words with colors of possibility—she eagerly plucked from them a blossom of identity for herself, placating one of the many questions she would wrestle with for years to come.

"Monday's child is fair of face,
Tuesday's child is full of grace,
Wednesday's child is full of woe,
Thursday's child has far to go,
Friday's child is loving and giving,
Saturday's child works hard for a living,
And the child born on the Sabbath day
Is bonny and blithe, good and gay."

The first time she heard the poem, Beatrice decided she was Wednesday's child. The old English nursery rhyme seemed to suggest that a baby born on Wednesday would have a life full of grief, regret, and distress. With hidden satisfaction, she identified herself immediately as Wednesday's child. Given her calamity of woes, she must have been born on a Wednesday. Filling the empty shell of her identity with such tiny bits and pieces grasped from fantasies gave her some insulation, softening the world of rejection and cruelty as she dragged her oversized sack of sadness through each day.

Fear was a constant companion as, with each soft step in her attempts at silent invisibility, she tried to avoid a blow to the head, a handful of hair yanked from her scalp for no other reason than merely existing and drawing breath. Denied simple opportunities from the moment of unwanted conception, her life was dominated by inhumanity. Baptized in the water of bigotry, her early life was powered by gratitude for every small act of generosity, every smile or courteous word from a stranger. She devoured these crumbs of kindness, which lessened the pain of cruelty she experienced behind closed doors—hidden from the eyes of the outside world—and gave her hope and strength to rise above her circumstances.

Her adoptive parents named her Beatrice, a change of name in denial of their racist posturing. Her foundling name, Lim Chung He—the Korean equivalent of Jane Doe—was given to her by the orphanage that took her in at the close of the Korean War. An abandoned biracial toddler, found and delivered by American soldiers to a military hospital on a trail outside of Soule, this tiny, filthy, bony creature had missing patches of hair, a fungal infection, and a bulging stomach characteristic of malnutrition and dehydration. Nestled temporarily in warm arms, a place of safety that did not last long enough, she was passed to a medic for life-saving attention—one more mixed-race bag of skin and bones added to the multitude of orphans spawned in war and left to die of hunger, parasites, and disease, victims of prejudice that excused the abandonment of humanity tossed aside in the chaos of war.

Hatred and resentment hardened Korean people toward the perceived source of their misery. Trust in the United States and its military was marred by a preponderance of atrocities—some carried out by the US military and some by its allies. It wasn't until 1999 that the United States acknowledged, after a lengthy investigation by the Associated Press, that a 1950 letter from US Ambassador John J. Muccio authorized commanders in the field to adopt a policy of open massacre in such places as No Gun Ri and Pohang. US soldiers and seamen knowingly fired on civilian refugees fleeing North Korea. These refugees were particularly susceptible to attacks by the US and South Korean forces under the pretense that North Korean soldiers, backed by the Soviet Union and China, had infiltrated their numbers to orchestrate sneak strikes.

Hundreds at a time were killed, many of them women and children. "We just annihilated them," Norman Tinkler, a former machine gunner, later told the Associated Press regarding the massacre at No Gun Ri. The circumstance of war ripped away and discarded the simplest of everyday rituals of human dignity. Survival became the dominant quest for these traumatized people. The human character was morphed by desperation and the constant, erratic, nomadic movement to dodge or hide from the enemy. At the same time, their shattered trust caused them confusion as to who the real enemy was.

The memory of peace fueled their desire to restore all they had lost—a full stomach, a home, and shelter, the ability to experience joy. All that had been replaced by penetrating, earthshattering, thunderous explosions of bombs that left behind the taste of metal and the smell of burning flesh. The sound of rifle fire slicing through the air carried with it a screaming message of impending death.

Over a million civilians were killed and another million displaced during the Korean War, their way of life demolished as they were hunted by the enemy and inhumanly tortured for information they did not possess. For many, constant terror clawed into already wounded sanity as they watched hunger emaciate loved ones. It has been said that areas of Korea became devoid of trees. Deforestation occurred as leaves were torn from branches, bark stripped from trunks, and chewed raw.

A refugee possessing a tin pot at least had the power to create a difficult-to-digest soup. An entire family's support sometimes came down to selling a young girl's virtue in exchange for a Hershey chocolate bar or a soldier's rations—treasures of canned meat, fruit, and beans the dowry paid for the brief company of a young female family member, willingly given.

Many Korean women were trafficked by Korean brokers to work as prostitutes for the US military, often resulting in unwanted pregnancies. The birth of a mixed-race child brought shame to a family, regardless of circumstance, and crushed any prospect of future respect and marriage for its mother. Such babies were abandoned with the ease of using toilet tissue on a pile of excrement. This act of abandonment formed a sacrificial altar for restoring a woman's virtue and reprieve from a looming life of social exile.

One man infused with compassion saw the need for a solution to this humanitarian disaster and decided that his life's purpose would be to create that solution. A man of deep faith, Harry Holt took on the work of angels, kindness reflected in his eyes, which were shaded by bushy, unkempt brows. In the aftermath of the Koran War, his orphanage saved over three thousand abandoned orphans, many of mixed race, whose fathers were soldiers from the US or its allies.

In 1956, Harry Holt built his orphanage with his own money. Infants only a few hours old were left at the orphanage door. Some were delivered to him by military hospitals after their medical needs were met. He often discovered abandoned children on his frequent reconnaissance walks through the streets of Seoul, scooping them up to feed and give shelter. Later, he would find them adoptive homes in the United States.

The US practice of adoption by proxy made it easy for these children to be adopted. The adoption process was handled by civilian volunteer liaisons. Once given authority, they would represent adoptive parents and help them navigate the complexities and necessary paperwork with phone calls and photos. They checked the integrity of the information provided by these perspective parents to the best of their ability.

Mixed-race children were rejected in Korean society. They were not allowed to hold a job that a pure-blooded citizen could have. Girls were often condemned to prostitution to survive. Boys were forced to a life of servitude, bearing heavy loads and delivering materials on their backs. Treated as the lowest class of society, they were called "dust of the streets," equal in status to stray dogs, to be kicked and spit upon as they begged for food.

Harry witnessed all forms of racist brutality toward mixed-race children. Their futures of abuse were displayed before him and tore at his heart. His mission was fueled by a fierce passion for saving the lives of as many of these children as possible, and his work was carried on long after his death by the Holt International adoption agency, which became known worldwide. Harry worked at his purpose until the day his heart stopped beating, eight years after founding his orphanage.

Lim Chung was one of the mixed-race orphans who went to adoptive homes in the United States. She entered the orphanage at about three years of age—a guesstimate, with consideration for stunted growth caused by malnutrition. The day she entered the orphanage became her official birth date; her true origins are lost in the ashes of war.

An infant knows its mother's scent, the sound of her voice, the beating of her heart as it grows in her womb. Upon birth, it experiences feelings of familiarity and safety as hunger and the need for warmth are satisfied. When the attachment is broken, emotional trauma begins with the search to find or replace that missing connection; the result is often depression, post-traumatic stress disorder (PTSD), and feelings of inadequacy as the child moves forward into an identity riddled with questions and doubts.

Physically, Lim Chung began to thrive in the orphanage environment, where she was kept warm, fed twice a day, and bathed weekly. However, she mainly sat in secluded spaces whenever possible.

She manifested apprehension in a cloud of mistrust, pulling away when anyone would try to touch her. Over time, she noticed that children occasionally disappeared, never returning. She did not understand that they left to join adoptive families. Their disappearance made her uneasy; she worried that the comfort she was currently grateful for might be temporary.

The tiny orphans were taught to pray before every meal to the best of their ability. Harry was a man of faith and encouraged faith in those in his care. Once a week, the orphans were gathered and taught songs about how God loved them and gave His life for the world. The idea of worshipping an unseen being was difficult for these small children to understand and caused them great confusion; singing, however, put flickering smiles on their faces. Their benefactors and house mothers encouraged goodness and placed a big emphasis on obedience.

Korean house mothers were employed to clean, change bedding, do laundry, prepare meals, and give baths. A few of the house mothers harbored a personal, bigoted dislike of their mixed-race charges and took delight in tormenting them with frightening stories of demons and devils. Seeing the children's frightened eyes as lights were turned out, several of these women stealthily made their way outside under cover of darkness one night to scratch on the windows. House-mothers-turned-thespians whispered, "Devils are coming to carry you all away." The giggles of these tormentors were drowned out by terrified squeals and cries. Karma reigned the next morning when saturated bedclothes in several cots had to be replaced. Frightened children wet their beds.

For many of these orphans, their first Christmas in the community was a misunderstood and traumatizing event, especially if they had received that gift of terror from those misguided house mothers—the orchestrated moments of nighttime fear when imagined demons and devils clawed at windows and walls, threatening to carry the children off to places of hellish torment.

Excited whispers echoed throughout the orphanage as children were gathered in the recreation room. "Santa is coming!" "He's coming!" "Listen!" No one under five knew who or what Santa was or why he was coming. The jingling of tiny bells and loud, bone-chilling bursts of "Ho, ho, ho!" could be heard as the door suddenly flew open and slammed into the wall. In the doorframe stood a giant creature dressed in red. Its long, curly white beard matched its long white hair. Slung over one shoulder, it lugged a considerable sack, possibly stuffed with kids it had already snatched along its way.

Suddenly, several dozen terrified children scattered about the room, stumbling over one another like tiny, inebriated elves, screaming their little lungs out, eyes streaming with tears as they searched for escape. The scene was chaotic. Santa could see they were not happy to see him and, realizing that his good intentions were totally misunderstood, immediately went into damage control. He and several volunteers who accompanied him grabbed the sack from his back. They dumped its contents in the middle of the floor, randomly ripping away Christmas wrapping paper to expose toys donated for this failed celebration.

Soon, efforts to soothe the traumatized children began to succeed. They settled into silent, tear-streaked curiosity as they fumbled with newly acquired toys. Lim Chung's unsuccessful attempt to escape through a window that she was too short to open increased the flow of her blinding tears. The huge Santa, navigating toward her through the chaos, removed his artificial beard and spoke gently, hoping to ease her fears. Christmas, the birth of Jesus, and Santa Claus were new to Korean culture. As the child took in the deep blue eyes, the gentle voice, the outstretched hand that held, as an offering, a doll dressed in pink, she was instantly transported to another dimension, and her terror subsided. That memory brings her comfort to this very day.

It was 1957, and she was about five years old when, a few weeks past her second year in the orphanage, a band was placed on her arm, claiming her for an adoptive family in the United States. Harry Holt was relieved to find Lim Chung He a home. She was approaching the age of exclusion from adoption set by the Korean government. Since her date of birth was uncertain, he wanted nothing to jeopardize her flight to America.

Lim Chung He's adoptive mother chose to name her Beatrice. Her name was Estelle, and her middle name was Beatrice.

Estell

Chapter

2

Estelle

The year was 1906. Silk curtains danced in the breeze of an early spring day in Kentucky. Eight-year-old Estelle welcomed the sun's warmth as it streamed through her bedroom windows. Volumes of thick, dark curly hair cascaded down her back, held in place by satin bows to match the color of her dress; she had bows to match any color dress she chose to wear. Shaded by long, lustrous lashes, her deep blue eyes contrasted dramatically with her translucent porcelain skin. The only child of Anthony and Charlotte Huff, Estelle was a gorgeous girl. With each passing year, she became increasingly aware of the attention she drew on entering a room. All eyes fell on her, and this attention made her feel powerful.

She clutched the teddy bear her father had given her after one of his long business trips. It was handmade and jointed, allowing it to be arranged in any pose she desired. She loved how it could sit on a perfectly designed child-size chair at her matching painted table. The teddy bear sat and looked her straight in the eyes. It was her first memory of what became many expressions of her father's love, which he bestowed with a warm embrace, a whispered endearment, and a kiss on the cheek—all suffused with the scent of his cigar and a whiff of brandy.

Looking out her window, she watched the African American workers scattered about the vast estate spread out before her. They were pruning branches of huge dogwood and red maple trees, a ritual performed every spring, digging up the rich, dark soil to sew new crops and nurturing existing plants that would soon burst into exotic colors. They continually manicured the landscape to pristine perfection.

Every detail of Estelle's life exuded perfection. Her wardrobe—created in textures of thick, rich satin in floral colors, transparent silk from the Orient, painted with intricately detailed butterflies and winding patterns of chartreuse greenery with accents of deep pink and violet blooms—was a wardrobe envied by every young girl fortunate enough to be invited to share in the entertainments and festivities that took place in her perfect world. Estelle's collection of porcelain dolls was another source of envy. Several wore woven wool trimmed in mink, with matching hats and miniature handmade leather shoes. Each doll came dressed in the costume of a country her father had visited.

Estelle's world was perfect in appearance only. From the moment of her birth, she was breastfed on her mother's milk of bigotry. Charlotte despised the poverty she was born into. She tried to shake off the shame of growing up poor and the memory of things she had done to survive. But shame clung to her with the foul stench of guilt.

Wielding a sword of chiseled beauty to slash through the barriers of gender and birthright stamped with generational wealth, Charlotte succeeded in detaching herself with precision from her humiliating circumstances by changing her mood and style to fit the character of whoever was pursuing her at the moment. When she met Anthony, though, her surrender was immediate. She abandoned what had been a search for true love, exchanging it for a life of wealth. And the cost was a price she desperately and willingly paid.

Charlotte's entrance into Estelle's room was accompanied by a fragrant scent of perfume and a confidence powered by everything that adorned her body—from elegant dress to extravagant jewelry—all of which concealed her inner insecurity. Her dark hair, as always, was coiffed to perfection. While a secret tapestry of hidden truth and self-loathing lay tucked behind her mask of expensive cosmetics and clothing, she successfully constructed her self-confidence with the acquired golden armature of wealth.

She glided into Estelle's room carrying several extravagant dresses. "Which one do you want to wear tonight, Estelle? These just arrived—aren't they exquisite?" There was no excitement in Estelle's eyes. She slid off the brocade settee and ran her fingers over the gown made of teal-colored satin. "This one is fine," she said in her southern drawl, without emotion or gratitude. Disappointed at the child's lack of interest, Charlotte flung the dresses onto the satin bedspread. "Estelle has always been hard to please," she thought. Having grown up wearing rags herself, she would have died to possess one of these dresses at Estelle's age.

As an infant, Estelle threw increasingly worrisome tantrums. She would angrily smack the face of whoever was holding her, whether it was her nanny or her mother. Her parents avoided disciplinary action that might launch the child into one of her tantrums. As soon as a tantrum appeared imminent, her mother immediately flung her into the arms of the nanny, who endured the pounding and scratching without complaint so as not to lose her job.

Anthony Huff adored his daughter, tantrums and all. He would deny her nothing. Estelle's bedroom suite was filled with the most expensive furnishings available, from tapestry curtains to hand-woven pastel wool carpets from the Middle East. A handmade, intricately carved dollhouse occupied one corner of the room, large enough for Estelle to stand up in, and a life-size rocking horse, carved and painted in pastel hues, was among the elaborate gifts he had given her.

Raised in an orphanage, Anthony loved Charlotte for giving him the family he had wanted all his life. He adored how she clung to his arm when they walked in public. Charlotte's stunning beauty drew attention wherever they went, adding inches of height to his self-esteem.

At sixteen, he had struck out on his own, determined to do whatever it took to become rich. Somehow, he managed to amass a fortune in a coal mine that revealed a gold vain, becoming an instant tycoon. He married his first wife for her small inheritance, which helped catapult his business venture into success and even greater wealth. Plain, frail, and sickly, she could never manage to hold a pregnancy to term and died trying.

Twenty-four years younger than her fifty-two-year-old husband, Charlotte loved him for the simple reason of gratitude. Young and beautiful, she clung to her short, aging husband with a death grip from the moment she stepped into his mansion and saw an opportunity to gain wealth and security. Occupational opportunities for women were limited by their economic class. Charlotte came from the lowest class, just above a formerly enslaved person. She was a "working woman"—the term used for women who worked at a factory or service job and prostituted themselves in the evenings for extra income to support a fatherless home.

Charlotte was willing to do whatever it took to become the wife of this wealthy man. Within days of discovering she was pregnant, he wed her with absolute joy in a quiet, secluded ceremony. The year was 1898, the same year Estelle was born. Though he had only known Charlotte for a few months, denial sent to the back of his mind any suspicion he might have had about deliberate planning on her part; he kept it there in the darkness and did not let it interfere with his happiness. Now, he would have a beautiful wife and an heir.

Anthony and Charlotte were a perfect match in their past circumstances, each accepting the other's flaws with passive contentment. But sudden wealth changed Charlotte; she became condescending and arrogant. No longer poor, she bathed herself in luxuries she had once only dreamed of. He compensated for what her husband lacked in stature and youth by giving his wife everything she desired. She, in turn, took every advantage of his generosity and the joy it gave him to see her delightful acceptance of it all. She exclusively wore a costly perfume because Anthony said he loved how it smelled on her,

Estelle, too, loved the fragrance her mother brought to every room she entered.

In 1907, Estelle's Aunt Clara, her mother's younger sister, came to live in the household. Estelle was only nine, but she soon discerned her aunt's true nature. She watched as Clara cast jealous eyes on Charlotte. More than once, she met Clara in her mother's room, running her fingers through Charlotte's elegant clothes and eyeing her jewelry. Estelle saw Clara admire everything that belonged to her sister—including her sister's husband. Estelle grew to hate her aunt. The hatred became mutual.

When her mother died, Clara had nowhere to live. As her sister, Charlotte could not deny Clara shelter now that she was alone—fatherless and motherless—but Charlotte was uncomfortable with the fact that her sister, five years younger and even prettier than herself, represented competition. With a sigh of resentment at the situation and her husband's encouragement, she accepted responsibility for her sister—but only with conditions.

Even though Clara had to suffer the constant flaunting of her sister's good fortune and be ridiculed by Charlotte at every turn, she accepted the offered position as manager of the household. Her pay would be room and board, and her responsibilities would be to oversee servants and supplies and the everyday running of the house. Charlotte required her to wear a uniform and apron that covered her body from neck to toe—to hide her figure from Anthony and ensure that guests knew Clara was more a servant than a relative.

While boasting about how she was contributing to her sister's wellbeing, Charlotte never tired of reminding Clara of her generosity. Overwhelmed by jealousy, Clara's resentment of her sister turned to hatred, and her hate soon grew to encompass her niece. She seethed at Estelle's look of contempt every time their eyes met. Clara's choices were driven by daydreams that luck would bring her a better life. Her sister had succeeded. So, she promised herself that she would.

Charlotte oppressed the servants. When she was a child, her family was considered lower class, but African Americans comprised the lowest class of all. Because of her family's poverty, they lived in a dilapidated shack close to the Black community. Her father, Henry, was a tall man with a rugged complexion. His once-handsome face had become puffy and bloated, and his belly bulged. Decades of drinking cheap alcohol had ruined his liver and saturated every other organ in his body, including his brain.

A racist bigot, he leaped at any opportunity to bully an African American man, woman, or child. Doing so alleviated the self-hatred and shame he felt at his position in life. This anger transference was a medicinal salve for his psyche that made him forget the miserable hopelessness of his life and his future. Cheap alcohol or moonshine sucked up his paycheck, even though, at times, it meant his family would go hungry.

Henry died during one of his drunken rages while assaulting a Black woman. When the woman's brother stepped in to defend her, Henry fell backward in his drunkenness and hit his head on a rock, cracking his skull. He died immediately. Soon afterward, the young Black man was dragged from his family's shack and lynched. The town never blamed the drunk—his white skin bore the evidence of his innocence while the brother's dark skin confirmed his guilt—regardless of evidence, facts, or witness accounts such as the woman's swollen face, bruises, torn skin, and ripped dress, or that a loving brother was performing a protective act.

Charlotte grew up with the same ideology and mindset as her father, having witnessed and absorbed his bigotry all her life. The unbroken generational chain of hatred added another link. She believed that her father had been killed unjustly and was comforted by the knowledge that the young Black man had died for his misdeed. She willingly carried this generational hatred into her newly acquired position of wealth.

Estelle looked on and learned to emulate her mother's cruelty—forging yet another link in the unbroken chain of hatred. Estelle was taught from birth to believe that her white skin made her superior, and it was her God-given right to act so. Although African Americans were no longer enslaved, they were still burdened by a bigoted heritage of subservience and cuffed in unbreakable chains of oppressive poverty.

Estelle would be physically violent toward servants for the pure comfort of following her own prerogative. She once kicked over a bucket of soapy water, drenching a servant her age as she scrubbed the floor. The girl looked up at her with confused, questioning eyes. Estelle started screaming at her to mop up the mess, accusing her of deliberately getting Estelle's shoes wet. She shouted racist words as she yanked at the girl's hair, bringing her to tears, and then ran from the room, also crying, to find her father and tell him her version of the story. That same day, Estelle's father fired the young servant, along with her mother. Estelle watched them go with a smile of satisfaction as they passed her with tear-stained faces.

Estelle's character did not improve over time. She was beautiful, blessed with thick, naturally wavy hair and piercing blue, almond-shaped eyes, but her loveliness was only skin deep. She continued to search for any occasion to be cruel to Black servants. During one of these acts of cruelty, she looked into her mother's face and saw a smile affirming her malicious actions. She loved giving her mother a reason to smile affectionately at her. She loved her mother completely.

Until she was almost ten years old, Estelle lived a life of privilege in the center of her small universe—indulged by her adoring parents.

Chapter

3

All is Lost

Estelle's parents decided one day to take a holiday—a rare trip without their daughter to celebrate their anniversary. They planned to go on a short shopping extravaganza and bring her gifts when they returned. But they never returned. On February 16, 1907, a train on the newly electrified New York Central Railroad's Harlem division rounded a curve and jumped the tracks at Woodlawn Station, resulting in 20 deaths and 150 injuries. Charlotte and Anthony were two of the passengers killed in the accident.

When she learned of her loss, Estelle's heart was impaled with soul-crushing grief. Her Aunt Clara's only show of emotion was in her hands, which were shaking with excitement as conniving wheels began to spin in her mind. Planning how she would justify what was about to happen, she wasted no time in seizing an opportunity to take possession of what she felt was owed to her. Estelle was the only heir, and Clara was, after all, Estelle's only surviving relative. She was entitled to take charge of the family fortune for the niece she would now raise.

Estelle's world crumbled immediately in a dizzying earthquake of chaos, abuse, deception, theft, and loneliness. Clara entered a relationship with a lawyer who, seeing the vastness of Estelle's inheritance, guided Clara into legal possession of everything, leaving

Estelle penniless. Estelle watched as Aunt Clara sold her parents' furnishings, their paintings, even her beloved China dolls and dollhouse, her couture dresses and shoes. Clara had plans for Estelle—she would not be needing fancy dresses where she was going. She told the child that these things needed to be sold now that her father could not provide for her.

Estelle watched as Clara wore her mother's gowns and adorned herself with her mother's jewelry. She smelled her mother's perfume on Clara when her aunt entered the room. One day, Estelle began frantically searching for the teddy bear her father had given her, unable to find it in her now sparsely furnished room. When she asked Clara where it was, her aunt ignored her. When she asked again in a tone of desperation, Clara turned to her and screamed, "Leave me! I have no time, nor do I care or know where it is." Which was a lie.

Clara knew where everything had been and how much she received in payment for each item that gradually disappeared from the house. Estelle was staggered by the enormity of her loss. She felt life sucked from her, leaving her an empty shell of flesh and bone. Every breath that entered her body was expelled as a dark, thunderous scream of rage. She was frequently locked in her room to vent her helplessness and grief.

She could only watch as servants carried out pieces of her world, exchanged for money Aunt Clara shoved into a red velvet bag with gold tassel drawstrings—a bag that had belonged to her mother. She could only watch as each piece sold was driven away. Estelle managed to snatch several photos of her parents and hide them away in secret places so that they, too, would not disappear. Then came the day when Clara told Estelle the house had been sold. As she stood in the hollow shell of what had once been her universe, another wave of grief engulfed her, and her sobs echoed through the empty mansion.

Clara was anxious to rid herself of responsibility for Estelle now that she, Clara, had legally taken possession of the girl's inheritance. She picked out a plain white dress and ordered her niece to wear it. Estelle did as she was told, moving her body mechanically, her mind in a fog of grief and uncertainty. Her photos were safely hidden inside her dress. She sat in Clara's newly purchased Model T Ford and watched, tears streaming down her face as the car moved away, and her childhood home receded until it disappeared from sight.

Clara was unmoved as she glanced at Estelle in the rearview mirror. The car drove for hours through the night and finally parked in front of a brick building with a massive cross above the entrance. Telling her young passenger to stay in the car, Clara got out and knocked on the door. Soon, a woman in a black dress and white bonnet opened the massive, creaking portal. Estelle nervously watched the interaction between the two.

Sister Agnes was expecting Clara. As their only contact had been through letters, Sister Agnes looked Clara up and down, assessing the woman in front of her—pretty, well-dressed, and adorned with diamond earrings and a matching broach pinned to her suit jacket.

"Where is she?" asked Sister Agnes.

Clara nervously explained, "Unfortunately, sister, I have not had a chance to explain to the child the circumstances of her placement with you. She is troubled and violent at times. She is having a hard time accepting the fact that she has lost her parents and is now orphaned. She is from a needy family but tells everyone differently. She is even confused about her last name. I am certain that, with patience, she will do better."

Then, with a thin-lipped smile, Clara handed the nun a velvet bag containing a large amount of cash and said, "This donation should help the orphanage and its needs in abundance." A smile of surprise crossed Sister Agnes's face as she shoved the velvet sack into the folds of her gown. "Bring her to me," she said. "We will break her circumstance to her."

Clara pulled Estelle out of the car. Her eyes brimming with tears, the child looked frightened and confused. She struggled to resist her aunt's hold on her, but Clara shoved her closer to Sister Agnes, who grasped Estelle's arm like a vise.

"Her name is Stella!" Clara said as she tossed a cloth bag containing several dresses, a sweater, and a winter coat at her niece's feet. She had made sure nothing of quality or couture was in the bag—nothing to suggest Estelle came from wealth—having purchased the clothing from a mercantile store close to her childhood home in preparation for this very moment. She had covered her tracks of betrayal to the last detail.

"My name is Estelle!" her niece screamed at her. "I hate you!" she cried through gritted teeth, her eyes flashing with angry disbelief. Clara turned away, smiling with relief and satisfaction at finally reaching her goal. Unloading her dead sister's brat was the finale.

"No!" she yelled loudly to Sister Agnes. "Her name is Stella!"

She did a victory sashay to her car. Looking back into her niece's tear-soaked eyes, Clara gave her a look of satisfaction as she cruelly stripped the girl of her last and dearest possession. "Her name is Stella," she yelled once again, with a snicker. She slid into her car in utter contentment and drove away. Sister Agnes dragged the girl inside and shut the massive wooden door behind them. Estelle was now an inmate of a Catholic orphanage for girls in Louisville, Kentucky.

Estelle held onto her grief—her one dependable, solid connection to her mother and father—as she replayed comforting memories. Her parents drifted through her dreams—the scent of her mother's perfume, the rustling sound of satin, the smoothness of her pearls, the delicate feel of silk, and the softness of velvet against her skin as she melted onto her mother's arms; her father's lingering scent of cigar smoke and the smell of his nightly glass of brandy on his breath as he kissed her goodnight.

Her grief ebbed and flowed, often replaced by waves of thunderous rage at the memory of Clara's crimes, of her stolen inheritance and betrayal. Anger and resentment would become a crimson thread of memory that bound her to the loss of the only two people she ever loved. Estelle's ability to trust was stripped from her, both physically and emotionally, by theft and abuse. Her young life became a vacant cave, devoid of the love, support, and guidance she desperately needed.

Without the means to repair her damaged and broken psyche, she would carry that carpetbag of misery and resentment toward Clara until she breathed her last breath at eighty-six years of age.

Sister Agnes immediately loathed the newly acquired orphan. Anger shot from the girl's face at anyone who offered her friendship, and she would turn her head to avoid having to make eye contact or even acknowledge another person's presence. The sister introduced her to everyone as Stella, aware of how much it angered her. Determined to break the girl's spirit, she played with the child's emotions, thinking how entertaining it would be to hear that final snap of resilience. The only remaining piece of her identity was her name, given to her by adoring parents. She clung to it, turning emotional claws of rebellion against anyone who would take it from her.

One day, shortly after she arrived at the orphanage, Estelle defiantly refused to respond to Sister Agnes when she addressed her as Stella. The nun grasped her arm in a painful grip, spun her around, slapped her in the face with a heavy, open hand, and shoved her against the cold stone wall. Leaning forward, she looked directly into Estelle's shocked, frightened eyes. No one in her past had ever assaulted her—she had been the one who victimized and assaulted others.

Sister Agnes breathed into her ear through gritted teeth, "Your name is Stella. Is that clear?" Pressing harder on the girl's chest, she pushed her back into the unyielding wall and glared at her with threatening eyes. "Tell me your name!" grunted Sister Agnes as she pressed harder on the thin chest with her huge hand, making breathing painful. Estelle's fear extinguished her rebellion, and in a hoarse whisper, she answered, "My name is Stella."

Sister Agnes immediately pulled her hand away with a satisfied smile as she heard the silent snap of Estelle's broken will. At the same time, yet another segment was added to Estelle's crimson thread. "Good," said Sister Agnes. "We have come to an understanding. Stella, you have a lot to learn. This is now your home. A daily quota is required from you to ensure a bed to sleep in and food to eat."

At the time, Stella had no idea what a quota was, but she was soon introduced to its meaning about the slavery of child labor. Stella was taught to crochet with a hook and needle and care for the rolls of yarn required to create baby blankets, bonnets, socks, and sweaters encased in satin-lined gift boxes. Several of the nuns were assigned as teachers. The children must hastily learn a trade to increase production of these products, which were sold to popular brand-name stores in support of the orphanage. Insufficient speed was met with harsh discipline. The nuns used long, flat wooden paddles to whack fingers and hands that failed to meet the daily quota.

Child labor was hidden from public awareness at the turn of the twentieth century. Social programs were practically nonexistent. Those who lacked empathy preyed on the vulnerable, victimizing children of various ages, forcing them to sit on long benches, hunched over as they worked frantically to fend off abuse that would be directed at them if they failed to meet a quota and so increase bring in revenue for their abusers.

Over the next three years, Stella erected a mental shrine to the ideology of her mother, adopting the same love of material luxuries: the same arrogance, racism, and hatred. She trusted no one and refused every offer of friendship with condescending conceit. She relived each unjust, humiliating moment of those three years with unrelenting anger. The first time she was told to scrub the rectory floor, she brought back a shattering memory of herself as a child, taunting a black-skinned servant.

In a fit of rage, she refused, shouting, "No! It's nigger work. I won't do it!" Sister Agnes was called to handle her. After failing to control Stella's hysteria, Sister Agnes grabbed the wooden mop handle and slammed it across the girl's back. As Stella screamed, the mop handle broke in two. Sister Agnes held her down until Stella's body relaxed. Sister Agnes commanded her to mop the floor or be locked in the disciplinary closet, a frighteningly dark, rat-infested room with nothing to sit on but the floor.

Stella got on her knees with heaving sobs and scrubbed the floor as her tears mingled with the mop water. Unmoved, Sister Agnes once again heard the satisfying silent snap as she stood over Stella. The broken handles of the mop made loud, clanking echoes as they bounced off the marble floor. Sister Agnes turned and walked away.

Estelle reinforced the emotional fractures and purple bruises with rods of iron will until the day she could walk out of the orphanage's prison-like walls. Multiple times, Sister Agnes attempted but failed to beat the existence and fear of God into Stella. Each time, Stella remained unmoved and absent of tears. If there was an all-powerful God, she hated Him for not being powerful for her circumstances. She refused to be commanded to believe the nuns' idea of faith and morality; she was done with restrictions, rules, quotas, and constant claims that she owed the orphanage for every bite of food, every blanket for warmth, every comfort she was made to feel she didn't deserve. Her calloused, bleeding fingers proved that she had earned it all.

Stella grew into a striking young woman. She became self-confident and more defiant with each passing year. At thirteen, she looked years older. Sister Agnes decided it was time to give Stella an ultimatum regarding her future. "Become a novice," Sister Agnes demanded as she sat behind her large desk, "and eventually a nun. You will no longer be required to work on the manufacturing bench. You will be sent to novice training and then have an opportunity to dedicate your life as a nun. If you refuse, you will be required to leave and no longer benefit from this sanctuary. Since you have no family, no home, I assume you will take my offer."

Within seconds, Stella stood up to look down at Sister Agnes and reply, without hesitation, "No! I choose to leave! I won't stay, and I do not want to see your face one day longer than I have to. And as far as me benefiting from you and this place, it is you who benefited from my aunt years ago. I am not an idiot. I saw the velvet bag my aunt shoved in your hand the day you dragged me through those doors. The money stuffed inside that velvet bag was my money from my stolen inheritance."

Sister Agnes jumped to her feet, her face flushed with fear at hearing the truth, which she thought had been kept secret all these years. "Leave, you ungrateful liar! Once you leave, don't come back." Sister Agnes was shaken. It had taken a few years for Stella to realize the nature of the transaction that had taken place on the night she was delivered to the orphanage. The velvet bag that disappeared into the folds of Sister Agnes's habit was the same velvet bag she had often seen Aunt Clara stuff money into as her family's furnishings and her belongings were sold off.

Sister Agnes's brain immediately began working to explain away Stella's revelation that the nun was paid to get rid of an unwanted child—a revelation that could destroy her. She thought no one except Clara and herself knew of the small fortune contained in the hidden velvet bag. Clara had assured her that all had been done legally. But what if it was all lies? What if the money she took and hid from the church orphanage was discovered? With shaking hands, she removed money from the velvet bag, leaving a tiny fraction of the original amount.

On the day Stella left through the massive orphanage doors, Sister Agnes handed her the velvet bag, holding it high for all to witness, and loudly explained, "This was to be given into your possession when it came time." With a smile of relief, Sister Agnes felt vindicated. If anyone questioned her about it, she had given Stella what belonged to her. It was never plundered, only safely stored on Stella's behalf. Along with the velvet bag, she gave Stella a train ticket to Lexington, Kentucky. The farther away she was from the orphanage, the greater the distance between the truth and lies about her past.

Stella angrily ripped the bag from Sister Agnes's hand, aware of the nun's false display of innocence. The enormous wooden door slammed shut behind her with finality, ending a chapter in her life that added three years of trauma to her original loss and betrayal. As she walked down the cobblestone street, she looked up at the blue sky and whispered, "My name is Estelle!"

Chapter

4

The Oldest Profession

At first, after leaving the atmosphere of oppression that permeated the orphanage, Estelle was exhilarated by her freedom. Still, she soon felt an even heavier burden of loneliness and vulnerability related to her youth and gender. In the absence of protection and wisdom, she became easy prey. The year was 1910. At that time, Lexington was famous for its red-light district, and Estelle unknowingly stumbled right into it.

She felt she was being watched and looked up to see a man leaning in a doorway, smoking a cigarette. When their eyes met, he quickly looked away and flicked his cigarette to the sidewalk. Later, another man approached her. He had followed her to see if anyone accompanied her; confident he had correctly pegged her as a prostitute, he held out money as he approached. She turned and screamed at him, "Leave me alone!" This drew attention, and he hastily scurried away.

Naive and reckless, she spent money on cookies, sliced cake, and fruit she had not tasted in years. In her wanderings, she encountered a tiny boutique where she bought a pink and baby blue dress that made her think of the colors her mother wore and a wool jacket with a collar trimmed in fur. She was unaware that the shop clerk charged her double the price and then deliberately short-changed her. The clerk did not like being treated with the condescending attitude of someone she assumed was a young whore. She had to be a whore. Where else would she get that kind of money to spend?

Drunk on her newfound independence, Estelle initially gave no thought to tomorrow, but soon her tiny fortune was gone. The reality of her situation came into full view and hit her with ground-shaking force. Broke, hungry, and homeless, she sat down on a cobblestone curb under a streetlight as darkness started to soak up the daylight. It wasn't just men who mistook her for a prostitute; several ladies of that profession eyed her competitively, jealous of her youth.

As she sat under the streetlamp, raindrops began to tap on the cobblestones around her. She drew the fur collar of her new wool jacket around her neck for added warmth. The air held a cool crispness of fall, triggering a deep sense of fear in Estelle as panic about her future survival intensified. A sudden flash of anger filled her as her circumstances became more apparent with each drop of rain.

"What's your game?" demanded a female voice, interrupting her sad reverie. The woman sitting at her side thought this young girl must already be in business—her clothes looked expensive. Estelle, in turn, thought this woman was wearing way too much makeup on her aged skin and bright red lips, which supported a lit cigarette.

"Where you from?" she questioned Estelle as she blew out cigarette smoke.

"From an orphanage," Estelle snapped.

"You an orphan?"

"Not anymore. I left."

"So, where're you going," the woman asked.

"Why is it any of your business?" Estelle loudly responded.

The woman raised her palms in a gesture of calmness. "Hey, just thought maybe you might need some help is all," she replied. "You are too young and pretty to be out here alone. I was once exactly where you are right now."

Estelle became more agitated as the rain increased its tempo, and the drops fell harder. She was getting soaking wet. "Come with me," the woman said loud enough to be heard through the now drenching rain, "where it's warm. There will be no business for me tonight in this weather." Having no other options, Estelle got up and followed the woman.

Estelle visually processed the contents of the woman's room when she switched on the light. The smell of perfume filled her nostrils, triggering memories of her mother. "My name is Belle," the woman said. "Take off your jacket. Hang it on this chair to dry."

Brightly colored embroidered curtains trimmed in beige fringe framed the windows. Handwoven Persian rugs covered the floors. The bed was covered with a satin-covered down comforter and matching pillows.

Belle was on her knees, kindling a flame in the small fireplace set into an intricately carved mantle. "Sit," said Belle as she pointed to one of the winged armchairs facing the fireplace. Belle's closet doors stood open, revealing dresses of every color—some with rhinestones, feathers, fur. Estelle had not seen such lovely possessions since her mother died. She closed her eyes and breathed in the scent of the perfume that filled the room. "Belle is being way too kind," Estelle thought to herself as the conversation continued. She was right; Belle wanted something from her. Mistrustful of everyone, thanks to Aunt Clara and Sister Agnes, Estelle was comfortable but suspicious as she sat surrounded by her past's quality textures and colors.

"So, you are an orphan? Do you have any means of supporting yourself?" Belle asked. Estelle stayed defiantly silent for a moment before shaking her head.

"I have an offer of employment," Belle said.

"Will I be able to have things like what is in this room?" Estelle asked as her eyes assessed the contents of Belle's apartment.

"Honey, at your age and with your looks, absolutely! I will teach you everything you need to know. If you agree to my terms, you can stay in that room over there," Belle said, pointing to a closed door at the other end of the apartment.

"My terms are these: once you break in, I will get a small percentage of what you make." Estelle did not understand what "my terms "and "percentage "or "make" meant. All she heard was "room" and "bed" and the possibility of restoring some of what had been stolen from her. "My name is Belle," she went on. "I run several brothels here in Lexington."

Explaining the difficulty of overcoming the circumstances of Estelle's gender, age, and lack of education and strategically poking at the girl's pride and bigotry, Belle held up thc unattractive options of working in sweatshops or as a servant for a wealthy family, painting an honest picture of the disadvantages of being a woman in a man's world. She also pointed out the powerful ammunition Estelle possessed—her body and youthful figure. "Men want what you got, and why not make them pay for it?" Estelle soon agreed to an internship with Belle, under whose guidance she became proficient at what they referred to as "selling pieces of her time."

After filling her stomach with Belle's bread and cheese and toasting their new partnership—her first small glass of white wine—Estelle nestled her head into the satin pillow, reminiscent of long-ago familiar softness. Belle looked down at Estelle's flawless complexion as she slept. She was pleased with this new acquisition of her collection of willing girls. Known for running an orderly operation in a very disorderly business, she worked hand-in-hand with Lexington law enforcement, which could be persuaded to look the other way when needed. Many officers in the police department were, after all, customers of her establishments.

Belle was said to let her girls keep most of their earnings. They were the attraction—the bait—that drew drinking men to her establishments; she made most of her money through liquor sales. One of her brothels had three stories. The bottom floor was for regular blue-collar workers who wanted to enjoy Belle's liquor. The second floor was for limited engagements with her girls and liquor consumption. The third floor had a back entrance for well-to-do clients who needed assurances of safe, clandestine encounters—men who had one concubine they saw regularly and exclusively to limit their chances of contracting a sexually transmitted disease. These included politicians, clergymen, and married men of wealth.

Belle's brothels flourished until the late 1910s when Prohibition forced her to shut down. Before her downfall, she was well-liked, even beloved, for her generosity. She thought of her girls as family. Toward the end of her life, Belle died of cervical cancer, addicted to heroin.

Estelle fits perfectly into the world of compensated, emotionally detached relationships. She became highly sought-after at only fourteen years of age. Wealthy men competed for her exclusive companionship. After the childhood losses she had suffered, Estelle promised herself that she would never be vulnerable to anyone ever again. Whatever she had to do in the future, she would never trust another for her survival.

At the first episode of vomiting, Belle knew Estelle was pregnant. Her condition was kept secret, and Estelle continued working—servicing her client, the elder son of the local police chief—until the pregnancy could no longer be hidden. He immediately denied paternity, and Estelle gave birth alone. All previous attempts to abort the pregnancy had failed. The experience of childbirth contributed emotional torment to a life already traumatized by earlier events. The child whose birth tore her body open with unbearable pain and the men she held responsible for her pain were added to her collection of hated objects.

It was easy to rid herself of her unwanted child in a place and time when having multiple children was an asset. They brought additional income as child laborers working in sweatshops and guaranteed their parents someone, to care for them in old age. A family accepted Estelle's newborn girl child, swayed by her promise to provide financial compensation whenever possible. Although she gave them her contact information as assurance that the promise would be kept, Estelle had no intention of honoring it. As soon as she could, she returned to the only occupation she knew. Such was her inability to connect with anyone emotionally that she felt no regret whatsoever over giving up her child. Vowing never again to experience the agony and pain of childbirth, Estelle had three more aborted pregnancies.

When Belle's business was eventually shut down by Prohibition, many of her girls took to the streets to continue their trade, most of them becoming infected with gonorrhea and syphilis. A few girls found husbands and left the business altogether. Estelle was forced to leave the small bedroom in Belle's establishment, which she had decorated in colors and fabrics recalled from her childhood memories. She settled on a businessman to marry. In time, her husband's abusive pressure to have a child became more than she was willing to accept in exchange for the comfort and protection of a home, and Estelle left the marriage. Over thirty years, she married two more times. Between marriages, she worked as a chorus line stripper and, for a short time, had a carnival act in which she wrapped a python around her shoulders.

She picked her third husband, an army private, for his monthly allotment check. She married him just days before he was shipped overseas to fight in World War II and made her home in California military housing. Months later, she received a telegram that he had been killed in action. Estelle was single and on her own once again.

The passage of time took a toll on Estelle's self-confidence. Heads no longer turned when she entered a room. She began to feel the devastating invisibility of every woman in her late forties whose value and self-worth are measured by her attractiveness. Estelle's chances of finding someone to support her financially were beginning to dim when her biological daughter, given away decades earlier, tracked her down. Mildred Rose had grown up with multiple adopted siblings. Her childhood was a chaotic, painful soup of dysfunction.

Her daughter is now thirty-four years old. Accompanied by her naval officer husband Rod—a tall man with a ruddy complexion—

Mildred went to meet her birth mother. During her childhood, Mildred had created a fantasy of a loving mother who was searching for her and would appear at any moment with open arms and affection. As an adult, she regretted all the missed years of mother-daughter companionship. She could not have imagined that she would be met by her birth mother with emotional detachment and annoyance.

Estelle assessed Mildred from head to toe and felt her confidence soar as she compared her daughter's looks to hers. With heartbroken disappointment, Mildred watched Estelle's attention focus on Rod as they explained that he had been recruited for a job in Seattle with US Customs and Immigration. Estelle's eyes never left him, and he stared right back, shocked at how youthful Mildred's mother looked—but after all, she and Mildred were only fourteen years apart.

Estelle was still slim—much slimmer than his wife—and attractive. Her red lipstick was alluring, especially as she constantly ran her tongue across her lips while staring fixedly at him. Estelle immediately became determined to do whatever it took to acquire this man for herself. She could read a person easily, and her chameleon-like personality could adapt as needed to help achieve her goals. Silk stockings with black seams that ran up the back of her legs emphasized her ankles, which were tiny compared to Mildred's, and her low-cut neckline exposed her ample bosom. She brushed an arm or leg against Rod at every opportunity. After months of suspicion that he was seeing someone, Mildred followed him one day and caught the two of them in a tryst. Her shock at the devastating revelation that the other woman was her mother ended the marriage in that instant of heartbreaking realization.

Estelle felt no regret or guilt whatsoever at the enormous betrayal—one of her many character flaws. Immediately after the divorce was final, Estelle proclaimed that she was pregnant with Rod's child. She insisted on a hasty marriage before her pregnancy started to show—a trick she had used in the past to pressure a man into marriage.

Rod complied, excited to start a family. He bought property on the outskirts of Seattle, in rural Snohomish County. Rod and Estelle had moved and started building a home before he realized there was no child. His anger and resentment over the deception trumped any affection he may have felt for her. Remembering Mildred's goodness and loyalty as a wife, Rod regretted the actions that had led to their broken marriage. He hadn't allowed her to be a mother before he invited a Jezebel spirit named Estelle to enter a portal opened wide by his lust.

The deeper he looked inside himself, the greater the emptiness. He filled his hollowness with self-loathing and depravity, setting in motion years of indiscretions and affairs and a pornography addiction. As Estelle saw Rod's interest in her waning, replaced by growing dissatisfaction and resentment, she began to fear that her financial stability was at risk. Once again, she cast about for solutions. Children meant alimony and child support if he left her—adoption looked like the answer.

Adoption attempts through local agencies failed multiple times during the application process. One problem was her age. She was fifteen years older than her husband. She had lied about her age on marriage certificates and lied about the fact that she had been married multiple times. She failed psychological testing and refused to give the agencies her medical records. She also had a past arrest record relating to one of her paramours, who died of stab wounds. Released from jail after forty-five days for lack of evidence, she had claimed that the blood on her clothing was from an embrace of shock overcome with emotion when she found the man on the floor of their shared apartment. Those who knew Estelle would have thought this unlikely to be true as she was not emotionally touched by anyone or anything.

During her search for children in need of homes, she read an article in the *Seattle Times* about Korean War orphans available for adoption by proxy. She saw two pictures—one of an eighteen-month-old boy and one of a five-year-old girl- tagged half-American and half-Korean. She sent the required deposit and filled out paperwork emphasizing her husband's navy service and present employment with the federal government. She let stand the lie about her age in her latest marriage license.

Chapter

5

Adoption

Lim Chung was now Beatrice, a new name in a new dimension of helpless confusion floating on currents of change. She missed the orphanage with its consistent, dependable comfort: morning breakfast was a slice of bread and a glass of milk; they had dinner meals of kimchi as the group of orphans sat at wooden tables and benches resembling picnic tables, which Harry Holt had built himself. There was a weekly bath and nightly use of the makeshift bathrooms lined up outside the bunk rooms, each one containing a recycled Folgers coffee can that perfectly fit tiny, round bottoms and served conveniently for nighttime use. She had climbed into her assigned bunkbed nightly, finding security in the daily routine.

Beatrice relished the gentle touch of Harry Holt's hand as he stroked her hair whenever he made one of his rare appearances. All the orphans would run to surround him, screaming, "Abeoji, Abeoji!" ("Father" in Korean) as if he was a rock star, and he would pick up random children to hug and show them affection with a delighted smile on his face.

All of that disappeared after a plane ride with a group of other orphans. When they landed at Seattle-Tacoma International Airport, the children wore hospital-like wristbands that identified them, listed their immunizations, and named the adoptive families who would meet them on arrival. Once claimed by her adoptive parents, she was taken to their Snohomish County home. Thus did Beatrice enter a realm of authoritarian control and years of physical and emotional abuse and torment.

Oddly, Estelle and Rod drew closer as they found sudden commonality in the satisfaction of abusive control. Beatrice was to call Estelle by her name. Nauseated at the thought that someone might think her husband was Asian, she did not want the public embarrassment of being mistaken for the birth mother of two Asian children. The children fulfilled her purpose of securing future financial support in case her philandering husband left her. When in a public setting, Estelle would loudly proclaim for all to hear: "These are my *adopted* children from an orphanage in Korea!" In her mind, she would garner admiration for her selfless generosity while providing an explanation to banish any possible misconception of her involvement in an interracial marriage.

Over time, Estelle's appearances with her adopted biracial children became rare. Similarly, Rod rejected being called "Daddy" or "Father." This made his subsequent sexual abuse of Beatrice as a child seem somehow less abominable.

The children were not allowed to speak their native language. If Beatrice mistakenly spoke Korean, she was punished with an open-handed slap across the face and a painful yank on her hair. She would then be required to sit in a chair and repeat, over and over, the English translation of the misspoken Korean word until Estelle was satisfied.

Andrew, Beatrice's brother by association of adoption from the same orphanage into the same home, was eighteen months old when he came to the United States. Upon seeing him for the first time, Estelle was horrified. He looked nothing like his adoption photo. She thought to herself, "He looks like a light-skinned nigger! He has nigger lips, too!" And for that, she despised him.

Adoption information identified Andy as half-American and half-Korean. To Estelle's chagrin, the American half happened to be African American. Her conniving backfired all over her bigoted narcissism, disrupting her plan. Her frustration at being trapped into raising a Black and Asian mixed-race child spurred physical abuse. Estelle rained abuse upon him and Bea all their young lives. They did not escape the bigotry and hatred Harry Holt had tried so hard to save them from.

To avoid some of the abuse his sister suffered, Andy learned what was acceptable and what was not. Estelle started each episode of abuse in terrifying, unexpected anger that turned her face red and caused her bloodshot eyes to protrude from their sockets. Andy would scamper to find a place of hoped-for invisibility, this time squatting under the kitchen table and watching as a flood of profanity erupted from the terrifying pit of Estelle's mouth.

The episode began with Estelle mumbling unintelligibly while she filled the kitchen sink with water. As the transformation continued, her profanity became guttural. She grabbed Beatrice by her hair, dragging her to the water-filled sink. Then, lifting her up by the seat of her pants, she plunged the girl's head underwater. Repeatedly, she held the child submerged until the pain of water-filled sinuses and the desperate need to breathe brought forth a sputtering admission of guilt for whatever imagined transgression the voices in Estelle's head had conjured.

Waterboarding was Estelle's torture of choice. In this instance, it was the imagined theft of a piece of candy. Delving into the forbidden stash of Estelle's expensive hand-dipped milk chocolates was not worth the terrifying risk of discovery for either child. Still, their innocence did not spare them from punishment.

Once Estelle was satisfied with a coerced admission of guilt, given in exchange for the ability to breathe, she threw Beatrice to the floor, where she lay crumpled like a wet rag doll. Her terrified little brother crouched under the kitchen table, watching through chair legs that somewhat resembled prison bars. Andy's eyes met hers as he reached out and gently touched Bea's hand in a gesture of comfort while she lay coughing painfully in a puddle, water, and snot running from her nose to form an air passage to her lungs. Estelle threw a towel at Beatrice, commanding her to mop up the water; without concern, she walked out of the kitchen. Bea raised herself to her knees and, in mechanical motions of overobedience, mopped the floor dry.

While Estelle's torturous behavior was horrifying, Rod's abuse, though quite different, was equally despicable. In their innocence, children never question when blame is laid at their feet. They pick it up and clutch it to their chests, taking ownership, accepting anger and punishment as somehow deserved, trusting that abuse is normal, defending their abusers while hiding their bruises and torn orifices—a gesture of loyalty—hoping only to satisfy their desperate hunger for love and acceptance, vulnerably confusing abusive touching with affection.

As Beatrice matured, Rod's abuse intensified. She continued a silent endurance that pounded her body with trauma. Rod was confident that the girl's naivety and fear of more intense attacks assured him of her silence. Bea was prohibited from having friends or outside contact except during school.

Estelle and Rod were bound by the adoption agreement, which stated that both children were required to attend school. But for Beatrice and her brother, school was merely a continuation of the emotional abuse they suffered at home. They were forced to dress in oversized clothing purchased from Salvation Army grab bags for a couple of dollars a bag. They were two of the few Asian students enrolled in the school. The fact that they showed up wearing cast-off clothing gave school bullies a target and a surplus of piercing verbal bullets—hurtful taunts that riddled holes in what little self-esteem they possessed—"Rice ball," "Gook," "Jap." As Bea and Andy walked the school's halls, these cruel children laughed and ridiculed their clothing while pulling the corners of their eyes up to imitate slanted eyes. Teachers often turned their backs to avoid having to intervene.

Estelle's bigoted hatred of Andrew intensified as he grew. She beat him and Beatrice with the buckle end of belts when yard work quotas were not met, always aiming at backs and legs where clothing would hide bruised and broken flesh. She would write notes to the school excusing them from participation in gym classes so that the marks on their bodies would not be exposed when changing clothes in the locker room.

Accusations of imaginary theft continued to spur undeserved punishment. One morning, Estelle dragged Andy to the school bus stop. When the bus arrived, she pulled him up the steps, loudly proclaiming to a busload of his peers that he was a thief, and forced him to say, "I am a thief," as she held his head up with a painful grip of his hair. He could not contain his tears of shame and humiliation. The bus driver sat in shock at what he was witnessing.

Continuing to sob, Andy made his way to a seat next to his sister; his head bowed as he tried to tune out the whispers surrounding him until the bus arrived at school. Bea and Andy waited until the bus was empty and then rose to leave. The bus driver stopped Andy to offer a handful of tissues and a hug. This unfamiliar kindness overcame the little boy. The bus driver hoped that his hug would channel strength to this broken child and somehow compensate for the abuse he had just endured.

Soon afterward, on an icy, snowy day, Beatrice and her brother found several boys waiting as they exited the bus after school. After the bus drove out of sight, these bullies started taunting Andy and calling him names. He and Bea kept their heads down, avoiding eye contact. The lack of response bored the bullies; they grabbed Andy and quickly pulled off his oversized pants, then tied his shoes together and tossed pants and shoes over the sagging electrical wires above. As they ran off, they laughed in triumph at their bullying and the further humiliation of their defenseless target.

Draping her coat over Andy's shoulders, Bea tried to give him warmth as he walked home along the icy streets without pants or shoes. Nothing could mend his humiliation as, with each frigid step, he carried his broken spirit to the place they called home. The pants and shoes hung from the power line for months afterward, a daily reminder of the painful incident.

Bea's young life was empty of peace as she tiptoed daily through Estelle's emotional minefield, uncertain what might trigger an explosion of abuse. Constant attacks crashed through the oppression. She struggled not to give in to the insanity that kept knocking at the door of her clarity. Andy imbued her with purpose. Her little brother needed her to protect him and give him strength. Rod had threatened to make Andy his whore if Beatrice exposed him to anyone. She sacrificed herself to protect her younger brother from Rod's depravity.

What little sleep settled on her was haunted by dreams that echoed with marching boots slamming into the ground to the unmistakable rhythm of war, a tune of suffering and death. She could not talk to anyone about these dreams, which repeatedly took her to a place of darkness and shards of broken glass surrounding empty eyes. This dream revisited her nightly, morphing with time into nightmarish detail, its sounds and textures becoming more profound in their context of terror. After this dream, she always awoke soaked in sweat.

Bea identified herself with the names and words Estelle screamed at her daily, even as Rod tore away her innocence along with her boundaries of morality. The word "no" was not in her vocabulary. The word "no" identified a choice she did not possess—to reject being the whore, the cunt, the gook, the Chink, the streetwalker, the bastard. Survival meant internalizing her shame, taking ownership of those words as descriptors of who she was, and accepting that the abuse she suffered was her fault.

Hope was a place Bea visited to escape her circumstances and dream of a better tomorrow, a place she went to in the dark of night. Darkness was a sweet place where her imagination could roam free, uninterrupted by anxiety. Each night, she unrolled a sleeping bag on top of a mat near the back porch door in case the dogs needed to relieve themselves. It was her responsibility to make sure they did not awaken Estelle. If any noise or disturbance woke her, there was hell to pay.

In the darkness, her imagination took her to a room that had soft, satin walls with sunlight streaming through the windows and a solid door that shut tight to keep her anxiety and misery outside. She would shut her eyes and create scenarios of joy—the discovery of a father who had been searching for her for years, a dream of belonging to a family in an atmosphere of love, one of her newfound father pulling up in front of her school, lovingly scooping her up and settling her into his shiny limousine while all her classmates look on in envy and watched them drive away.

The closet in her imaginary room was filled with beautiful dresses and bright, colorful ribbons to tie back a full head of long, pretty hair. In a glorious realm of childhood make-believe, there were dolls she could caress and serve a pretend tea with sweet cookies and spongy chocolate cake dripping with icing.

Suddenly, pain jolted her back to reality as she was lifted to her feet by her hair, and profanity assaulted her ears at the beginning of another day of misery.

Fifteen-year-old Beatrice stood at the edge of the wheat field one summer day. The golden crowns swayed back and forth, giving in to the intensity of the breeze. The wind was a gift that eased the heat of the sunshine beating down on her exposed, sunburned shoulders. As she stopped to wipe away the sweat, which stung her blistered hands as she wiped them on her dungarees, her searching eyes did not find the small figure of her brother in the field. Her assignment was to hacksaw and clear the growth of young alders. Too small to move them any other way, she would tie a rope around the trunk, tie the other end to her waist, and leverage her body forward to drag them the distance to a pile where they would eventually be burned. By the time this task was completed, she was exhausted and thirsty.

She and her brother were often locked out of the house, not allowed to enter until the day's quotas were achieved. Estelle usually left them for an entire day while she drove to town alone to shop and indulge herself at her favorite restaurants. Today was one of those days of self-indulgence. There would be no water or food until she returned to give them a can of Campbell's soup or a bowl of cereal.

After searching, she found her brother. His pants were missing, and he was rocking himself back and forth. When he stood, she could see that his underwear was bloody. He looked into Bea's eyes with a pained expression, his own eyes misty with unshed tears, processing the reality of what had just been done to him. Then he looked away, sat back down in the dirt, and began rocking back and forth again, burying his face behind his knees. Mumbling incoherently, he covered his head with his arms as if that might make him invisible.

Bea immediately knew what had happened. She looked up and saw a figure standing in the window of the closed-in porch. Rod sneered at the two of them before stepping back into darkness. Consumed with the need to achieve her quota, Bea had not noticed his return, and he had taken that opportunity to sodomize her little brother.

Seeing Andy's brokenness shook her to her core. All that she had given of herself to protect him crashed into inconsolable grief and self-hatred at the failure of her loyalty. She no longer owed silence to anyone. Anger solidified her hatred of the two people who controlled her life, the two people who indifferently manufactured misery for her and her brother daily.

Beatrice dove deep into memories of a time before Rod and Estelle had entered her life, memories of a time of emotional peace and daily routine when sleep was deep and singing songs brought a smile, when food tasted good, and touch was comforting. She sat down in the grass as grief overwhelmed her, letting tears wash away the pain of regret over her existence.

She had witnessed with envy the lives lived by other children in her school—the stylishly crisp, clean, colorful clothes that were sized perfectly for their bodies, the warm coats and gloves they wore in winter. She resented their smiles and laughter, which came so easily. She felt their disdain when she flashed a look their way and saw the parallel dimension to which she and her brother were refused entry. She was their exact opposite. She slept on the floor on the same mat as Estelle's two dogs. The mat was infused with their wet-dog smell—a smell that seeped into the ill-fitting Salvation Army clothes she was forced to wear. Her hair was missing in patches, exposing her pink scalp. This was rumored to be caused by lice.

The failure of her personal, sovereign promise to protect her brother from sexual abuse sent Bea deeper into the darkness of depression. Her mental and physical weakness, plus guilt over her perceived inadequacy, induced her to feel that she deserved the continued beatings and the insufferable, regular sexual assaults.

However, the next time Estelle screamed accusations at Beatrice during one of her psychotically fueled attacks, including that of being a whore, Beatrice's wall of silence shattered—it had become a silence that no longer carried any weight. She looked her tormentor in the eyes and screamed back at her, "Rod has been raping me since I was nine years old. If I am a whore, he made me one."

Estelle's fist stopped in midair as the words penetrated her skull. Deep inside the surviving sliver of her sanity, she already knew the truth. Still, the force of hearing it in distinct words slammed into her insecurities about her fifty additional pounds of body weight and her fear of aging.

Estelle's hatred of Beatrice instantly transformed. She was no longer a prop to ensure her self-interest of survival; she was a full-blown imaginary nemesis of a fifteen-year-old girl. Estelle was now eating the fruit of her own words. Her verbal accusations for over a decade became truth in her mind: Beatrice was a streetwalking whore and a liar. His denial validated Rod's innocence. It was easier to transfer her anger to the victim, condoning Rod's guilt after years of denying what she knew to be true. This gave power to her narrative of control over problematic situations she did not want to face. An agenda to rid Bea of her life, and ultimately Rod's life, was thus set in motion.

Chapter

6

Bondage

Estelle and Rod huddled together, Rod's arms flailing as if trying to capture airborne salvation after the disclosure of his actions or else juggling his sputtering words of denial. Estelle felt no affection for Rod or any other man. Their relationship was financial. Her jealousy of Beatrice went deep into the patchwork of her character, sewn together by unresolved anger, past abandonment, and cruelty-oozing scabs of resentment that refused to heal.

Having no concern whatsoever for Bea or her lost virtue, Estelle now saw the girl as an entity stealing her life. Her fear of losing Rod's financial support was stabbing holes in her confidence. In the past, her beauty and its promise of intimacy had been a slender jeweled dagger of control she could thrust into the lust of any man, married or single, who allowed her to suck monitory life from his pocketbook. Now, she felt unsure of herself.

Estelle's transition to senior citizen status was turbulent. The wrinkles reflected in her mirror stole her youth while hues of gray soaked up the rich color of her hair, confirming her mortality. She was devoid of any humanity and goodness that might surface, any possibility of inner beauty to give her value in old age. The sudden drumbeat of fear overtook her—fear of abandonment and its accompanying memories of overwhelming loss—gripping what was left of Estelle's sanity and drowning out any whispers of reason in her head. Her hatred erupted anew when she suddenly saw Beatrice as her competition for attention, no longer a hook she used to secure Rod's loyalty and monetary support. Estelle now had child rape accusations to hold over his head. Her next move was to eliminate the competition.

One morning, weeks later, she woke Bea and ordered her to put on the dress tossed on her bed. Today, she was going to marry the man who owned a restaurant Estelle frequented. She had spent years ensuring the word "no" was not in Bea's vocabulary. The girl's understanding of boundaries and honesty was twisted and painfully confused, especially by the experience of being forced to shoplift for Estelle.

The forced thievery left Beatrice emotionally drained, fearing the shame of discovery. The stress, etched on her forehead and upper lip with beads of sweat, pushed Bea to the edge of vomiting. Estelle would drive them into town to go "shopping." Estelle's intentions were clear to Bea on these occasions. She was never allowed on a shopping excursion unless she was to be used as a mule. Estelle could afford to buy whatever she wanted, in multiples, if she chose. But seeing Beatrice steal for her was a satisfying confirmation that the girl deserved whatever abuse was unleashed on her.

The Sears shoe department was Estelle's target of choice. She liked its lack of customer service and its proximity to the exit. Estelle would choose the shoes she wanted, set them down, and direct Beatrice to take them. The girl was to remove her footwear, slip on the chosen shoes, and walk out of the store in them—dragging her tiny feet to keep them from slipping off—to where Estelle would be sitting in her parked car. As Bea made her way through the parking lot to Estelle's Cadillac, she vomited several times from the stress of the ordeal.

"If you get caught, nothing will happen because you are a kid. Besides, you are a thief anyway," was Estelle's reasoning. Reflecting on her memories, Bea realized that her terror of getting caught indicated that she knew the difference between right and wrong, but she feared Estelle's wrath slightly more than she feared getting caught. It was a no-win situation: don't steal and suffer pain and punishment, or steal and run the risk of getting caught, knowing without a doubt that Estelle would throw her under her bus of blame. Bea rode home with cold feet, having sacrificed her shoes to Estelle's twisted mission of control.

Estelle's plan to rid herself of Beatrice was approaching a fait accompli now that she had found a willing man to take the girl off her hands. She had recently confided to her how lonely he had been since his divorce. Estelle suggested a solution to that loneliness when she, in turn, confided to him about her adopted daughter, who needed a more controlled environment than Estelle herself could provide.

Robert—in his fifties—was old enough to be the grandfather of his prospective bride. He had first seen Beatrice when Estelle brought her into the restaurant—ostensibly for a meal but mainly to allow him to inspect the "merchandise." He offered Bea a job washing dishes in his restaurant. Estelle immediately accepted this offer on the girl's behalf, setting up his access to her, taking advantage of the fact that her boundaries had been stripped away. He started with groping, cautiously exploring the territory in steps, examining options of control, weighing advantages against liabilities before accepting this silent, obedient, cowering creature.

For Estelle, her adopted daughter's usefulness had run its course. Pimping Beatrice out to rid herself of what had become an unwanted annoyance seemed justified. Estelle's concern was for Estelle alone—no one else mattered. Her focus for now was getting Bea out of her life—and, more importantly, of Rod's life.

On the agreed-upon day in 1968, Estelle drove Beatrice to the courthouse. The groom stood quietly beside her. She looked younger than her sixteen years; she was skinny, and her scalp had patches of missing hair. The white dress Estelle purchased at the local Wigwam did little to cover her abuse and neglect.

As Beatrice stood next to Robert with her shoulders hunched, he could see bruises on her arm and neck. She did not once make eye contact with anyone in the room and flinched at Estelle's every movement. It was apparent to the man who in moments would become her husband that this child was a product of abuse. Marrying her was even more justified in his mind—he was saving her from whatever cause or purpose lay in the dark heart of Estelle, whom he disliked more with every passing minute.

Estelle was confident that the marriage was final. After she pinched Bea's backside to prod her into answering when the judge asked, "Do you take this man?" the girl's "I do" was barely audible. Estelle signed her name to give her consent to the underage marriage. The judge performing the ceremony looked oblivious to the scenario being played out before him. He was in a hurry to finish his duty, receive his payment for services rendered, and move on with his day.

Before Estelle turned to walk away, she shoved a paper bag filled with Bea's shabby belongings into the girl's arms, giving her a look of evil satisfaction. Married at eleven in the morning, Beatrice washed dishes in her husband's restaurant by one in the afternoon.

When she became fully aware that she was not required to go home to Estelle and Rod ever again, she became euphoric. She attacked everything with newfound wings of freedom—freedom from the fear that had chewed away pieces of her mental health. Her self-esteem was a constant work in progress. She struggled to walk with her head erect. The confidence to make eye contact was not yet possible.

The degrading names branded into her psyche had created permanent scars. No amount of ointment in the form of positive thinking would completely heal them. But she now slept in a soft, warm bed. She chose what she wanted to eat and how much. She started to gain weight. Her husband threw away the clothes in the paper bag and took her shopping. For the first time in her life, she had new clothes purchased just for herself.

However, she was not allowed to choose what she liked. Her husband bought what he thought looked good on her, and her gratitude did not allow her to question his choices. She willingly settled into her new world, free—at least for a while—of the lingering anxiety that had floated ever-present in the past. Her husband's attitude suddenly soured in the instant when the sales clerk, looking at Beatrice, remarked to him, "How beautiful your daughter is." The shopping trip ended abruptly with a quick stop at the makeup counter to purchase lipstick, blush, and a pair of false eyelashes on the way out. He encouraged Bea to wear makeup, hoping it would make her appear older and lessen his embarrassment over their thirty-five-year age gap and the emaciated appearance of his new bride.

Bea's life experiences throughout her marriage were bound by her husband's determination to control her identity. Although she was comfortable and gratefully accepted the absence of constant cruelty and abuse, the boundaries she had so painfully learned after her adoption stayed in place—only speak when spoken, do not express opinions, do what you are told. She kept up a constant over-obedience in an effort to receive her husband's crumbs of acceptance.

Love was for people outside her world—couples in television commercials, couples walking together at the mall, smiling into each other's eyes while holding hands. The definition of love was twisted and distorted for her, but it left a twinge of confused recognition in her heart. Everything expected of her in marriage was carried forward from her yesterdays; there was no difference in physical compliance, except she received gentler treatment—no beatings or verbal abuse. Bea's confused interpretation of love was to offer obedience, loyalty, and gratitude—all of which were accepted by her husband as his due.

Robert introduced her to music—his music, but music nonetheless—and movies. He drew her into all the elements of his life—including cooking and baking. He taught her how to make the foods on his restaurant menus: preparation, execution and delivery, and presentation.

As years passed, she realized she was merely a possession he had added to his world. He denied her the opportunity to finish her education because he didn't want her to be in an atmosphere of independent thinking or the company of people her age. He clipped her wings at every opportunity. He chose the music she listened to and her clothes in his favored colors. He insisted that she always wear her hair pulled back and pinned up to make her look older and taller.

Robert also taught her the basics of business—bookkeeping, purchasing, and inventory control. He taught her to look customers directly in the eyes when speaking to them. She was oblivious to the attention she received when entering a room, but Robert consistently prodded her to walk with her head up and shoulders back; he demanded that she dress professionally, wear high heels, and apply full makeup every morning.

Over time, all his advice proved invaluable in her service to him, especially when she found herself responsible for their financial survival. He suffered from a heart condition and diabetes and then experienced a sudden onset of petit mal epilepsy. He decided it was time to teach Beatrice, now nineteen, how to drive. "You will need to drive to have a job. I can't drive you around in my condition." His driver's license had been revoked because of his epilepsy. Robert instructed her to change her birth year by four years when she went to apply for a driver's license. His comment regarding the deception was, "Now you can go into a bar with me." In truth, though, he wanted to project her as older than her years to relieve his embarrassment and discomfort.

Her husband's failure to obtain health insurance and the enormous medical bills that resulted forced him to sell his restaurant in the early 1980s. Bea suddenly became their sole breadwinner. She was fortunate that the internet and social media did not yet exist. Otherwise, it would have been difficult for her to embellish her age, education, and qualifications enough on job applications to get called for interviews.

She landed employment as a cosmetics buyer for a drugstore chain. Their encouraging comments when they offered her the job gave her head-up-shoulders-back-eye-contact confidence. "You have the looks, the youth, and buying and inventory control experience," they told her. She was thus successfully employed for seven years.

During all that time, Bea's marriage was based solely on her programmed sense of emotional indebtedness. Her husband was satisfied to have Beatrice in chains of gratitude for a life he credited himself with giving her, for the bruises she no longer bore, for the confidence she walked in, for the beauty that emerged under his guidance. He took credit for the personalized education he gave her, even though the cost was a controlling, dysfunctional, paternalistic relationship. He felt that she could only land her job because of his extensive tutelage.

Bea recognized that although Estelle was responsible for who she was on the inside, he was responsible for what the world saw of her on the outside. Her job enabled her to save money for the down payment and purchase of a house. While the transaction was made in her name because of Robert's unemployment, he claimed the house was his because of all he had done for her, and he drilled this into her at every opportunity.

She worked all day and came home to a dirty, disorganized mess. She would have to clean up and run a load of laundry before starting dinner because he wasn't feeling well. On the weekends, she had to witness his constant self-pity and listen to complaints about his unfortunate health problems, which he magnified to excuse his apathetic lethargy. He demanded that she not leave him alone. He would criticize the dinner meal if it weren't to his liking or if it was too spicy or not spicy enough. Her attempts to satisfy every detail of his expectations in the hope of receiving recognition or gratitude were met with indifference.

The emptiness of her life now overshadowed the indebtedness she had once felt, her gratitude replaced by slow-burning resentment and the longing for a more meaningful life for love and family. She yearned to smile from genuine joy, to know what happiness feels like, no matter how briefly. She saw happiness in coworkers' faces as she watched flirtations turn into engagements, photos capturing smiles of pure joy at a wedding or the birth of a cherished baby.

She envied others for their happiness while coming home each night to a life of emptiness, indifference, and obligation.

Chapter

7

Fight-or-flight

Stella and Rod blocked every attempt Beatrice made to communicate with Andy. She would call or stop by their house, hoping to see him, but she was always met with an unanswered door and unreturned phone calls. When a phone call finally came from him late one night in 1972, Andy, now sixteen, was almost unintelligible in his agitation. He said he had been arrested for attempted murder. The police had allowed him to make one phone call; assisted by a public defender, he had called her. Bea's heart leaped in her chest at the sound of his agonized sobbing.

When she reached the police station and was allowed to see him, all she could do was hold him as he melted into the familiar pain of abuse. Estelle was in the hospital in critical condition. Andy's attorney said she had been beaten with a chunk of two by four. She had a concussion and 160 stitches on her scalp. Her arm was broken in two places, and the police were waiting to see if she would survive before they decided whether to charge him with murder or attempted murder.

Bea's heart raced as she processed the immediate situation and what might happen to her brother. She was struck by the unfairness of life and slammed with intense memories of her time with Estelle and Rod and her old feeling of helplessness. To help Andy, she must pull back the curtain of darkness and expose the years of shame, fear, and abusive control. She would have to relive the terrible past. The only ammunition she had was her words of truth. The sudden overflow of emotion and suffering found release in the fight-or-flight response. To bring about justice, she decided then and there to bear witness to her and Andy's abuse.

"It was self-defense," she told Andy's attorney when she met him in the jail. Tears ran down her cheeks, and her words came out in a torrent as she related to him the years of sexual and physical abuse she and her brother had experienced. "Andy did this in self-defense. No one knows what he has endured, what I too endured."

The attorney assured Beatrice that a full investigation would be initiated, but a lot depended on Estelle pulling through. She saw her brother again before she left. He was broken, repeating how sorry he was and how much he regretted losing control. How well she understood what hurt him.

"I couldn't take it anymore. Rod wouldn't stop." She covered his lips, trying to tell him he needn't say another word, but he went on. "He wouldn't leave me alone," he finished in a whisper, adding, "Estelle wouldn't stop hitting me. She was screaming, 'Nigger, fag.' I saw the chunk of wood. I grabbed it, and then I blacked out. When I came to with it in my hand, she was on the ground."

Bea remembered multiple times she could have plunged a knife into Estelle's heart if there had been one close enough to wrap her fingers around. She understood acting on instinct to survive while blocking out the present moment—the tearing of the skin, the bruising of bones, the clumps of hair ripped out, the taste of blood from split lips, the abuser no longer human but an animal to drop before it claws you to death.

Tears connected the two of them as she hugged her brother. She was no longer the beaten down, bruised, terrified child. There were times in her past when she knelt and prayed to the God Harry Holt had told stories about—prayed passionately for Estelle to die. But her prayers were never answered. She now prayed just as passionately for Estelle to live.

On her brother's behalf, Beatrice stopped at the hospital to see how Estelle was doing. She was unrecognizable—her face swollen and bruised, her eyes blackened. Stitches went from the center of her head across her nose. A cast went from one shoulder to the tip of her fingers. Bea felt nothing except the hope that she would survive for her brother's sake.

As she turned to walk out, she saw Rod in the hallway. He looked shocked to see her. He did not appear as tall as she remembered. Perhaps it was because, as she stood erect in front of him, she was no longer a frightened child, hunching her shoulders, trying to be invisible. Anger made her refuse to be intimidated by his stare.

Hoping to somehow avoid blame by projecting his innocence, he immediately and loudly started to defame Andy, calling him an ungrateful, parentless child he had tried to save, and this was how the boy thanked him. Intense hatred burned through her as she returned his stare. There was no empathy or remorse in the dark eyes that looked back at her.

His perpetual smirk was no longer visible, but Bea's anger grew with every word that came from his mouth. Flashbacks began to hit her like a flock of attacking birds—images of what he had done to her and Andy for his own perverse satisfaction, calcifying her bond of protection, whatever the cost. There was nothing left to lose except Andy's freedom. She looked at his face, sweaty with fear that the assault on Estelle might expose his filthy depravity, and calmly said, "There is no time limit for statutory child rape. I look forward to testifying on my brother's behalf." Then she turned away and left him stuttering.

Beatrice prayed, unsure of the existence of the unseen entity toward which she directed her prayers. All she had was memories of her faith in Harry Holt. His sweetness exploded into a smile when his eyes met hers. The faith she felt in him extended to faith in the God he had told his orphans about. She prayed to his God to have mercy on Andy, to save the life of the miserable Estelle, to dismiss a murder charge, and to spare the life and future of her brother.

Estelle was subsequently moved from the intensive care unit. Bea's curiosity about the woman's condition and concern for her brother drove her to make another visit to the hospital. She was relieved to see Estelle sitting up. Harry's Jesus Christ became her God in that moment of gratitude.

Beatrice looked into the bruised and bloated face, the swollen, blackened eyes. Estelle spoke with difficulty, "I don't want your brother to come near me ever again! Do you understand?" Her attempt at using her familiar, intimidating tone failed miserably. Bea stood up and walked closer to the foot of Estelle's elevated hospital bed. As they made eye contact, Bea's anger exploded at the woman's arrogance. Seeing Rod had elevated her emotions and assaulted her nerves with terrible memories. Anger transformed her into an emotional animal.

"I have no sympathy for you whatsoever, you pathetic piece of shit. You deserve every blow your body receives. My brother and I didn't deserve a decade of your daily blows. Do *you* understand?

"I have given my deposition on my brother's behalf. I told the truth with details. And my guess is you won't have to worry about seeing either of us ever again, except, of course, in court. Hire a good lawyer because you will need one."

Unsurprisingly, Rod took a plea deal and was forced into retirement from his government job. After testimony provided proof of the abuse, Andy was placed in foster care. Because of his juvenile status, the record of his arrest was expunged.

Harry Holt's God continued listening to Bea's prayers. Her brother's court-appointed counselor became his foster parent. Bea watched her brother thrive in his new environment. His grades soared. He graduated with honors in his new high school. No one knew of his past. He told friends that his parents were dead. He dove deep into therapy, fighting his intermittent depression and PTSD, sparring daily with his feelings of guilt and self-criticism. Bea met with her brother often.

She loved to see Andy flourishing in all the positive ways she had hoped for him. He landed a job in a men's clothing store after graduating from high school. He dressed stylishly and bought his first car. It delighted her to see him developing a newfound confidence. But during several of her latest visits with him in the same little coffee shop, Beatrice was troubled by how distant and unsettled her brother had become. When she asked if everything was all right, he responded with a sudden rush of tears and nervously clutched his coffee cup. Emotion seemed to spill out from his anticipation of the pain his words were about to cause her.

"Sis, I know how much you love me, and please know how much I love you. I hope you will remember that when you hear what I have to say. I have decided to embrace my new life. My therapy is encouraging it. My healing and mental health depend on it.

"Every time I see you and spend time with you, I relive the misery I am trying to survive, especially the abuse to my body that I can't accept as a man. I look in your eyes, and the sadness is looking back at me. Flashbacks are collapsing the cornerstones of my recovery, causing me to feel that terrible desperation and overdose on antidepressants to make it through the night.

"I am so sorry, but I have got to leave my pain in the past, and you are part of my pain. The violations of our bodies connect us as one. I have to leave you behind. It is the only way for me to resurrect my life." Andy reached over to cover Bea's hand with his, hoping to channel his love through that touch, just as he had done when he was a child.

"I know you are not happy. Both of us are trapped in our past world of cruelty. Our memories continue to deny us life. I need to know you will walk away from the life Estelle chose for you and live a life of your own choosing. I will always hold the love and sacrifices and protection you gave me in a sacred place in my heart." He gave Bea a hug and kissed her tear-soaked cheek for the last time.

She burst into uncontrollable sobs as she made her way to her car through the pouring rain. She sat in her car as the rain pummeled the window, matching the downpour with the torrent of tears flowing directly from the pain that sliced into her heart. The only act of love she was now allowed to express toward Andy was her absence from his life. She tucked every word he spoke into the hole left in her heart.

The same blood did not run through their veins. Their connection came from an unspoken understanding of each other's painful parallel past. Beatrice envied her brother's ability to desensitize his emotions, see with clarity the initiatives he needed to take to improve his life and have the courage to act on them.

Bea focused on her brother's intuitive words about the unhappiness he saw in her eyes, the wisdom he personified, despite his own physical and emotional bruises, at the tender age of twenty. He spoke the truth, but she was miserable. Having given pieces of herself in misplaced loyalty lit by her own feelings of self-hatred, she had been willing to travel down a rabbit hole of continuing abuse to satisfy a debt she mistakenly felt she owed. Her brother's words set change into motion.

Grief replaced the relationship she'd had with her brother. Where once she had excitedly looked forward to biweekly coffee meetings with Andy—conversations and shared stories of small victories—empty spaces suddenly dominated her life. Her loneliness intensified. She walked through days of emptiness and spent sleepless nights drifting through nightmarish scenarios as the marching rhythm of boots thundered through the elevated pounding of her heart, leaving dark circles under her eyes.

Beatrice decided to seek therapy. It was a life-changing decision, a life-saving disruption of suicidal thoughts. Internalized memories emerged during therapy sessions. Bea was asked to remember a time of happiness in her early childhood. Closing her eyes brought images of snowy white clouds against a backdrop of deep blue. She was near a riverbank, laying on her back in the grass as it swayed in a light breeze. She watched a woman squatting beside a rock that protruded from the water; her skirt tied up high between her legs to keep dry. The woman slapped clothes against the rock, rubbed them with a small chunk of soap, and then pounded them with a slender stick until suds appeared. Beatrice watched the soap drift past with the current. The woman cast protective glances at Bea as she smiled with warm affection. The identity of the woman remains a mystery to this day.

At the therapist's request, Bea recounted her nightmares with as much detail as possible: "I think I am with the same woman. She and I are in a cave on a hillside. We are hiding in the cave. It is dark. I hear a sound like boots stomping on the ground—lots of boots. The next memory is soldered in dark green or brown, trimmed with crimson red. One of them is screaming at the woman. She is shielding me with her body, protecting me. The soldier has a sword or machete and starts striking her. The woman breaks into pieces of glass as the soldiers' march away with the same sound of boots slamming into the ground. I crawl through the broken pieces of glass. The woman's eyes stare back at me with no life in them. I begin to turn into shining glass.

"I have this nightmare repeatedly. As the years pass, it becomes more detailed."

When Beatrice recounted her time in an orphanage near Seoul after the end of the Korean War, the therapist hypothesized that the dream was related to something she experienced as a small child. When she researched the Korean War, the therapist discovered that many Koreans hid in caves and mountainous areas to escape attacks by Communist troops.

She told Bea, "Talking with you about your abusive past and how you survived it emotionally, I feel that at one time you were loved and experienced nurturing. Your nightmares of broken glass might have to do with blood. Blood is shiny like glass when reflecting light. You could have come into contact with blood as you crawled through what you describe as broken pieces of glass, where you also became glass. Bea, you are likely reliving a traumatic experience that occurred at a time in your childhood when you were too young to process it. Your suppressed memories can surface in times of trauma, stress, or sadness."

Some of Bea's questions would never be answered—she accepted that as part of her life. However, therapy helped her piece together bits of information to understand and at least partially answer many questions. It helped explain her emotional reaction when, having to handle raw meat in the process of cooking, panic arose in her at the sight of blood pooling at the bottom of the butcher's paper. Suddenly, there was clarity, but she still felt the confusion of incomplete closure. The therapist gave her breathing exercises to help her settle reactions triggered by PTSD. Though her nightmares gradually subsided, she experienced them intermittently for many years.

While undergoing therapy, Beatrice was mentally calculating how to break free from her marriage. She always stumbled over the question of how her husband would survive financially without her income. He was not yet old enough to apply for Social Security and Medicare. If she sold the house, how could he afford the rent? All the what-about questions kept multiplying, making divorce seem like an impossibility.

The more Bea compared the pros and cons, the less certain she became that freedom would be worth the cost. Her motivation for life-changing follow-through was exhausted. At times, lost in the anxiety of failure in every part of her life, she felt tempted to dive into an abyss of self-pity and disappear into peaceful nonexistence. Her world turned on its axis, continually erecting barriers to joy.

After seven years at her first job, Beatrice took a higher paying job at a commercial fishing ship, Chandler, an outfitter of Bering Sea crabbers, draggers, and southeast salmon boats—different products from her first job, but with the same inventory control system. She welcomed the change. The increased pay and new atmosphere lessened her desolation.

Chapter

8

Awakening

Beatrice clutched the rawness of her grief. She could accept the need and purpose of her brother's abandonment but was not willing to relinquish the pain of his continued absence. Nor could she let the passage of time dull her determination to honor his request for her to free herself from the shackles of past pain. Bea began to journey into a frontier of autonomous experiences she had always wanted but could not allow herself to have because they lay beyond a self-imposed boundary in a realm of undeserved freedoms.

As she added new experiences to her life, she created a connection to her inner self. She took long walks, went to movies, visited libraries where she borrowed books of poetry, wandered through art galleries, and dined alone at a restaurant where she chose whatever she wanted from the menu.

As Bea's weakness slowly metamorphosed into strength, she gradually empowered herself to break away from her husband's control. He could feel her self-confidence growing and his grip on her slipping. He made frantic attempts to tap into her insecurity and fear, which he had used as glue to keep her bound to him, reminding her with familiar words that he was the only person who cared about her. He tried to flip the narrative of their relationship to his advantage, telling her that he was the one sacrificing his life for her betterment, insinuating that she was not intelligent enough to survive without him.

He knew well how to navigate her insecurities to close any gateway to independence. His words had so often settled inside her, cuddling next to the demeaning, degenerate identity tattooed onto her self-esteem, instantly causing her to give in to defeat. But as maturity settled in, Beatrice began to draw levity into her life's journey and focus on moving forward, away from her defeated persona.

Bea's job gave her life a new purpose. She loved the commercial fishing industry and the daily characters that came, smiling, in and out of her life as they prepared for their voyages each season. The commercial fishing community—predominantly Scandinavian, Slavonian, and Native Alaskan—was connected by heritage and tradition as well as by harvesting the sea for financial and family survival. The community mourned the loss of every life and every vessel collectively. Bea felt the embrace of that family unit as she watched sons and daughters grow to become crew members and then captains of their own vessels. Grown to adulthood, they greeted her with the same smiles as when they had been small children running along the planking of the docks, dodging the fishing nets spread out for repair while crew members skillfully worked their nylon-wrapped net needles to mend tears in the webbing and conversed with excited optimism about prospects for the coming season.

Vessels varied in size from enormous processors to Bering Sea crabbers, from majestic seiners to smaller southeast Alaska gillnetters. Each ship's name and port were proudly painted on her stern. Beatrice watched from her office window as crew members climbed massive metal king crab pots while hydraulic cranes strategically stacked them on the decks of Bering Sea crabbers. Lives depended on their ability to balance and securely tie down the stacks to prevent shifting in rough seas.

Armed with aluminum baseball bats, deckhands on rotating shifts battled the encrusting ice that accumulated on crab pot, railing, and pilot house, which could cause the boat to become top-heavy and possibly roll over and disappear under the waves in the frigid waters of Alaska. Bea had sad memories of the familiar young and not-so-young faces of those lost to the sea, never returning to give their smiles to friends and those they loved.

Each workday, she ate lunch in a small café within walking distance of her office. To avoid accidental eye contact that might possibly lead to an unwanted conversation, she consistently looked for a secluded spot facing a wall. One day, two female voices in the booth behind her penetrated her curtain of privacy. One voice said, "If you are not happy, leave your situation." Another voice replied, "I am so afraid."

The first voice responded, "What could happen that would be worse than how your life is now? There are solutions for every situation life throws at us. If you have to walk away with the clothes on your back, it will be worth it. Waiting for the right moment is prolonging the inevitable. The right moment will always be now."

Beatrice bit into her sandwich as she chewed on the words she had just overheard—a private conversation ringing with inspirational truth. Asking and answering the same question for herself, she was reminded of her brother's words about promising to live the life of her choosing, not the life Estelle thrust upon her.

Fear, complex and multilayered, had dominated and paralyzed her for so long. But there was a tremendous longing growing in her. It was the substance of her worth, her universe of flesh imprisoning the pulsating heart of her self-confidence, that moaned to be freed from the monster of undeserving conscience. All too well, she knew the pain that accompanied every passing year of loneliness. Her agonizing desire to experience life began to build a scab that helped desensitize her to the programmed guilt brought on by her desire for freedom. Galvanized by the thought that nothing could be worse than her current situation, whatever the price, she used her fear as a catalyst.

When Beatrice told her husband their marriage was over, her voice shook with the effort to summon every scrap of courage she possessed. He became angry—not because she was ending a loveless marriage but because she would be ending his financial support. After she told him she would be selling the house, his voice cracked in panic, "How do you think I am to survive financially?"

Bea had thought through her breaking-away scenario in detail. She needed to walk away without leaving anything to eat at the delicate consciousness of her freedom. Avoiding eye contact and determined not to fail or deviate from the mission at hand, she said, "You will survive on 90 percent of the profits from selling this house and 90 percent of savings in the bank. I agree to pay your health insurance for six months—until the divorce is finalized. You will survive comfortably; you can apply for Social Security in a few months and Medicare afterward. I am walking away with almost nothing.

"I will always be grateful for your guidance and everything you have taught me. I have given you fourteen loyal and faithful years of my life. I have asked nothing from you in all that time. All I am asking for now is my freedom."

Bea's husband was satisfied with her offer, but he could not part ways without a final resentful comment: "The world will eat you alive without me." She gave no credence to his comment. It wasn't the world that was eating her alive; it had been a group effort on the part of people taking advantage of her unfortunate circumstances, each for their own purpose.

She took 10 percent of her savings account, placing it in a separate account out of which she would pay rent and buy furnishings for an apartment close to work. Until the divorce was final, her financial life was in limbo. The house sold quickly. Her husband immediately sold off the furnishings and pocketed the money. She was not impacted by any of his acts of animosity. Her freedom from guilt was bought and paid for, and he now had the financial resources to take care of himself.

Beatrice was grateful for the possibilities of life now unfolding before her. Once the divorce was final, the house sold, and the financial settlement completed, Bea searched for an affordable home—a sweet sanctuary—of her very own. She furnished it modestly, concentrating on a soft couch and a comfortable bed. After adding a few extras to make it homey—colorful wall art, fluffy couch pillows, an attractive comforter for her bed—she came home every evening to walls of freedom that cradled her and opened windows of light and contentment in her soul.

She would make a fire in the tiny fireplace and watch its flames on chilly nights. She would eat dinner in front of the television, and for the first time in her young life, she settled into a peaceful sleep each night. On Saturdays, she slept in, then walked to a café down the street for breakfast. Afterward, sitting in the park to enjoy the changing fall colors, she watched as the towering maple trees sporadically released their leaves, which pirouetted on gusts of wind until they ended their dance by settling gently on the ground.

The crisp air nipped at her cheeks and nose as tears filled her eyes—tears of indescribable gratitude for her present life. It seemed as if an unseen entity had embraced her with peace. Wiping at her tears as she walked home, she conceded her indebtedness toward the goodness and undeniable love and protection of what felt like a divine presence.

To find a connection to a spiritual center inside herself, Beatrice started attending church, sparked by sweet memories of Harry Holt. She deliberately chose a seat in the last pew at the back of the church, mainly to avoid unwanted invitations of friendship. She hated seeing the expressions on friendly faces turn into nervous half smiles when she replied, "Divorced," in answer to questions about her marital status and feeling their sudden pity for her fall from grace.

While sitting through a sermon on marriage as a sacred union—once married, all divorced couples go on to commit adultery for the rest of their lives in any new relationships—Bea felt convinced the minister was looking straight at her, adding spiritual failure to her brokenness.

Afterward, as she walked out of the church into the sunlight, the sun's warm embrace renewed her faith in her higher power's acceptance of her substance, and she decided not to succumb to anyone's judgmental assumptions about her.

Thanksgiving came and went. Bea's boss invited her for Thanksgiving dinner with his family, but she opted to spend the holiday at home alone. She could not shake the feeling of being an outsider and feared the invitation was motivated by pity. Holidays, she felt, were about family.

Christmas was serene and quiet. It was the first one free of disappointed hopes and expectations. She built a fire and watched the twinkle of lights on her small, decorated tree. As she listened to Christmas music, thoughts of her brother flooded her mind, and a wave of sadness washed over her as she remembered past Christmases with Rod and Estelle. Bea and Andy received no Christmas gifts; their birthdays were not celebrated. There were gifts under the Christmas tree, but they were only props packaged and wrapped with names made visible on gift tags for the benefit of any guests who stopped by. On those occasions, Bea and Andy were ushered into another room, the doors shut to ensure their invisibility.

After Christmas, the forbidden gifts were packed away and reappeared the following Christmas with new wrapping paper and ribbons as part of a fraudulent display of generosity. Every Christmas was sad and disappointing for both children as they witnessed the celebrations of the outside world. That did not keep them from hoping that maybe the next Christmas would be different. But it never was.

Beatrice deliberately stopped herself from turning the pages in her book of memories and brought herself back to the present. The holidays made her more aware of the absence of family. While her fellow employees became consumed with family obligations, gifts, and parties—all met with excited commitment and steeped in family heritage—these things seemed remote to Bea, especially the heritage part. But she now felt a world of possibilities opening before her, the most powerful of which were songs—poetry set to rhythms—with their ability to inspire and ignite sentiment and passionate emotions.

Another new world was books on self-improvement, survival and courage, and the sad, dark poetry of Edger Allen Poe. She gloried in making choices for herself instead of having choices made for her. This first Christmas on her own, in her new home, Bea made a simple dinner and sat in front of her Christmas tree, absent of any presents. Melting into the atmosphere of twinkling lights, she fell peacefully asleep.

Chapter

9

Reenter Estelle

In 1985, Beatrice received a phone call that shocked her. The voice on the other end sounded quavering but familiar. Sudden recognition made Bea's head spin with traumatic memories. The voice betrayed nervousness. "This is Estelle."

Bea immediately asked, "Where did you get my number?"

"Your husband, or rather your ex-husband, gave it to me." Estelle's breathing sounded asthmatic." I am calling to let you know that Rod passed away. He has been gone for some time."

Bea felt no emotion at the news. "What do you want?" she asked in a flat tone.

Estelle continued between short breaks of labored breathing, "I know it's been years, and the last time I saw you, it wasn't on good terms." Estelle's voice broke into sobs as she begged Bea to come see her. "I just want to talk. Please."

After a long silence, Beatrice responded. She agreed to a short visit. She was curious to find out why Estelle wanted to connect after all that had transpired. She was a bit shocked that Estelle felt she had a right even to ask to speak with her. The wounded child inside Bea, the one who endured unspeakable abuse to seek even a morsel of approval that never came, agreed to see her.

On a Saturday afternoon, Bea drove to the address where she grew up. When she turned into the driveway, gravel crunched beneath her tires—a familiar, dreaded sound from the past that would announce Estelle's return home. Both she and her little brother would nervously scatter to make sure their quotas of yardwork were done. Her heart began pounding. Her mind spinning as memories flashed past, and she questioned herself, "Why are you here? Why are you inflicting past misery on yourself?"

The house was in disrepair. Paint was chipping away from the siding, and the yard was overgrown with weeds. Sections of fencing had collapsed. As the front door opened, the nauseating smell of cat urine hit her full force. Estelle stood holding a black cat. At least a dozen more cats populated the room in various poses on the furniture and floor. What looked like cat excrement dotted the filthy carpet and furniture.

Estelle was unrecognizable. Her hair was in dreadlocked disarray, and when she stepped forward with the cat still in her arms, the smell emanating from her prompted Beatrice to back away as a wave of nausea overtook her. Clearly, Estelle was in severe mental decline. The scar visible on her forehead was a consequence of her past mistreatment of Andy.

"You look like life has been good to you," Estelle commented, squinting her eyes. Her grimace of a smile exposed several missing teeth, and her attempt to interject guilt with her comment on how well Bea seemed to be doing failed to prompt anything but instant resentment. "As if she had any part in my life being good," Bea thought, but she asked suspiciously, "What is it you want from me?" even though the woman's appearance spoke volumes of her need.

Estelle looked humble and defeated as she spoke, "I am about to become homeless. I am broke; Rod left me penniless." A tear ran down her cheek. "The bank says Rod took out mortgages I didn't know about and failed to repay. The house is in foreclosure." She burst into a flood of tears as she exclaimed, "They are throwing me out!"

There was panic in Estelle's voice as she repeated several times, letting the cat drop from her arms, "I am Stella all over again!" Beatrice had no understanding of some of the gibberish that followed, but it ended with, "I don't know what to do!"

Estelle's eyes exuded excruciating torment. Bea's own eyes widened as Estelle suddenly exclaimed, "You have to help me!" It wasn't "will you"—it was "you must." But Bea mentally pushed the words aside. Estelle's appearance—her brokenness and tears—pierced her revulsion and awoke her compassion.

"You are the only one who agreed to see me," Estelle sobbed. As she wrung her hands, Bea noticed the long, unkempt, dirty fingernails. The atmosphere of chaos and lack of fresh air began to choke Bea with an aching responsibility she didn't want to feel. She purposely let childhood memories flood her mind to validate turning her back on Estelle and walking away—the beatings, the cruelty, the scars she bore on her back and legs, the internal scars invisible to the outside world, the years of emotional solitude and unspoken shame that filled her life daily and robbing her of a relationship with her brother—a gaping wound that would not heal.

As she stood there in front of Estelle, she realized that even an empty shell of a human being—now consumed by the need to survive and feel worthy of love—was deserving of life and dignity. Looking at Estelle, she found no comfort or satisfaction in the woman's pathetic situation. All she felt was Estelle's hopelessness.

Beatrice tried to stay focused on problem-solving questions. What about Rod's retirement and his life insurance? Apparently, Rod had been having an affair. He signed his life insurance over to his lover. Forced to retire after the child rape investigation, he had taken his retirement benefit in a lump sum and spent it purchasing a house for the other woman, putting it in her name.

Bea had questions regarding Rod's Social Security, which Estelle should qualify for, and said she would look into it. She would try to find housing for Estelle. This house needed to be vacated for repossession, and that was going to be a huge physical undertaking.

Beatrice quietly took in the filthy, hoarded chaos surrounding her. Estelle clearly needed medical as well as mental health care. The wounded creature standing before her engulfed the resentful turmoil swirling inside her. Within hours, the weight of Estelle's world fell onto Bea's shoulders once more. This damaged woman was now back in her life. As she drove away, the misery reflected in Estelle's present life settled on her. Grudgingly, she told herself that every soul deserves a chance at redemption.

Beatrice spoke to the mortgage lender, explaining Estelle's situation. She asked for an extension on the foreclosure, enough time to plan for housing, to move Estelle and her possessions, and to find homes for a dozen cats.

She needed to free her time to accomplish the task ahead. Bea's boss allowed her to take several weeks of accrued vacation to resolve Estelle's situation. Her work family was just that to her—family—they accepted her request without requiring an explanation. They didn't judge her personal life. They offered help, but Bea graciously refused. She didn't want the secrets of her past to be revealed—it brought too much shame—and she wanted their respect, not their pity.

One thing at a time was the only way to handle the enormity of the task. Beatrice made the painful decision to let Estelle stay in her home temporarily, stressing the word "temporary." She hired a caregiver to bathe Estelle and wash and cut the dreadlocks from her hair. Bea bought Estelle new clothes that would ease dressing and undressing and threw away the rest of her daily wardrobe.

Beatrice stood alone in the living room of Estelle's house, assessing the situation and planning what she would tackle first as memories flooded every crevice of her mind. The combination of toxic smells and the chaos of hoarded garbage began to suffocate her. She franticly started to open windows and doors as labored breathing threatened unconsciousness.

She left the house to get her bearings, mentally and physically. Rolling down the windows of her car to feel the wind and filling her nostrils and lungs with fresh air, she made her way to a hardware store where she purchased latex gloves, industrial-size garbage bags, and dust masks, along with several bottles of water to hydrate herself. She also bought a small radio, hopeful that rock and roll music might help keep her floating on the surface of a depression that threatened to drown her in dark, demonic memories of what had taken place inside each set of four walls she labored in.

Day after day, she returned to the task of clearing out Estelle's house. Animal control officers came and removed the cats. Goodwill came and took all the unwanted furniture. She hired a junk removal company for everything else. The carpet was ripped up and hauled away, along with its disgusting fragrance of insanity. In Estelle's fireplace, which was filled with ashes the cats had used as a litter box, she burned Rod's extensive stash of pornography, much of it confiscated material from his Customs and Immigration job. Bea found this remarkably therapeutic. In a closet, she discovered an aged camelback trunk filled with news clippings and memorabilia from throughout Estelle's life. This she decided to take home with her to sort through later, along with multiple boxes of papers.

Beatrice completed the physical part of Estelle's financial divestiture. Now, it was time to find and gather information and original paperwork to secure Rod's Social Security benefits for Estelle. Since Rod had been in the military, Estelle was also eligible for his veteran's benefits. The goal was to make Estelle solvent and financially independent so that Bea could feel free from any further obligation.

Exhausted and hungry after a day of hard labor, she drove home, stopping on the way for fast food to share with Estelle. Of course, Estelle was unhappy with the meal. The French fries were too salty. The chicken wasn't cooked enough. Estelle's princess spirit was still very much intact. The caregiver left for the evening with her well-earned paycheck, and Bea fell onto her bed, exhausted.

When she awoke the next morning, she immediately shed her clothes and showered, angry at herself for having fallen asleep in her disgustingly filthy clothes, which smelled of sweat, cat excrement, dust, and anxiety. Her muscles hurt from days of lifting and shoving boxes on Estelle's behalf.

Her need to find housing for Estelle was now her driving force. She dove into the boxes of paperwork, looking for Rod's navy discharge papers, his birth certificate, his and Estelle's marriage license—everything needed to prove her right to his VA benefits. In a weathered address book, she came across a page with the name Mildred written on it—side marked "daughter"—and a phone number. In the same box, she found copies of a marriage certificate for Mildred and Rod, plus a birth certificate for Mildred with Estelle named "mother."

There were photos of groups of women wearing flapper hairdo styles popular in the 1920s, dressed seductively in see-through dresses and black fishnet stockings. An old, frayed photo depicted a baby girl dressed in an elaborately frilled dress—a huge bow holding back a cascade of dark, curly hair and a teddy bear clutched to her chest.

There was also a family portrait set in front of a giant white house with pillars adorning a massive porch. Next to the child was a woman, her body leaning into an older, mustached man. On the back of the photo, in childish lettering, was written, "Momma and Poppy."

The trunk contained dozens more photos, plus newspaper clippings of a woman arrested on suspicion of stabbing a man to death but released for lack of evidence. Bea was shocked and confused by the information she discovered in Estelle's trunk. Rod was married to Estelle's daughter at one time, who was a scantily dressed woman.

Chapter

10

Dark Secrets Revealed

Beatrice nervously dialed the phone number side-marked, "Mildred/daughter." The voice on the other end answered, "Hello, this is Mildred. Can I help you?" Bea explained who she was on the pretext of letting Mildred know about Estelle's situation. "Yes, I am aware of her situation. She called me six months ago to let me know Rod, her husband, my ex, died. She asked me to come see her. She must be out of her mind to think she has any right to my concern for her in any way! I told her never to call me again."

Beatrice apologized for bothering her. "I didn't know she had already contacted you." Mildred was civil, but her underlying dislike for Estelle was evident in her tone. Bea finally asked, "Are you Estelle's daughter?"

Mildred's immediate reply was, "Yes, she had me when she was fourteen. She gave me away to be raised by someone else. I was ready to forgive her abandonment because of how young she was at my birth. Then, when I found her in my thirties, she seduced my husband. He left me for my mother. I wish I had never found her. But then, again, perhaps she did me a favor. Regardless, there are boundaries that we do not cross as humans. She was my mother, but she will forever be dead to me."

Bea thanked Mildred for her time and hung up the phone. "Wow," she thought, "what a shocking revelation!" But there was more. Bea found marriage certificates for Estelle's four separate marriages. Her date of birth was different on each one, and not one matched her original birth certificate, which was also among her papers, yellow and discolored with age. By the following morning, Bea had found the paperwork she needed to initiate the process of accessing financial benefits for Estelle and reclaiming her own privacy and peace.

Beatrice attacked her mission with the quiet energy of duty—her perspective being, "Everything happens for a reason"—not necessarily for Estelle but for herself. She was coming to terms with her resentment and anger for past misery and immeasurable loss—the fourteen years she spent emotionally locked in an arranged marriage instigated by her adoptive mother. Estelle had gifted Bea's husband the keys to lock her servitude in place after imprinting on her psyche an abundance of lasting memories that would be triggered in her daily routine.

The pain of Bea's past was a tapestry woven with a crimson thread of gritty texture that she felt with every memory. The years that followed, during which her husband and educational mentor taught her the basic life skills she lacked and the fundamentals of financial survival, eventually prepared her to walk away from the marriage, but only after she had paid him in full of years of faithful loyalty, service, and gratitude—and a tidy sum of money.

Her act of helping Estelle starkly contrasted Bea's strength and integrity with Estelle's abandonment of goodness in favor of ruthless cruelty. It allowed her to let go of any fear that the decades of neglect and abuse might have caused elements of Estelle's flawed character to be imprinted on her own and be reflected in Bea's actions.

Her financial follow-up on Estelle's behalf was soon successfully completed. Estelle now receives Rod's Social Security benefit in her bank account each month. His VA benefits were successfully applied for, and Beatrice hoped she could soon find Estelle her own apartment or perhaps a place in a retirement home.

But Estelle was declining mentally with each passing day. There was a disconnect in her eyes. She was argumentative regarding any request, especially for baths and daily grooming, but her experienced caregiver graciously handled the brunt of her anger. Bea made a doctor's appointment for her. There was an urgent need to find a medical or pharmaceutical solution for Estelle's outbursts of anger and her deep depression. It would be difficult to find retirement housing for her in her current mental state. The doctor ordered blood work and an MRI.

Amid her mental decline, Estelle had a good day of temporary clarity, and Beatrice decided to bring out some of the contents of the camelback trunk. As she laid out each item for Estelle to see, recognition lit up her eyes—the photograph of a little girl and her parents in front of a mansion, the scantily clad women draped in feather boas. Bea asked inquiring questions regarding each image. Estelle unashamedly pointed to herself with childlike pride. Each marriage certificate and newspaper clipping prompted Estelle to have a clear memory of their personality, faults, and bias that told a story of Estelle as the perennial victim.

In this way, they went through Estelle's life, from her early years to the present. Beatrice learned about Estelle's mother and father and how she lost them; the mansion she lived in; the Black servants in attendance—her comments about each person tagging her bigotry—the theft of her identity and inheritance by her aunt; the Catholic convent and the forced child labor that is extinguishing any faith or spirituality. If there was an all-powerful God, then she laid the blame at his feet as the architect of all her misery and loss. The most shocking thing for Bea was Estelle's admitted years of prostitution—her only option because of her youth and gender, and the loss of her social status and wealth and the education they would have afforded her.

The man who was Mildred's father denied his paternity because Estelle was a whore—even though she was exclusively *his* whore. She hated the child she had given birth to, blaming the newborn for disrupting her life. Abandoning her child to be raised by someone else was the solution that allowed Estelle to continue her livelihood and her responsibility to the child she still was.

The more Estelle spoke about and recalled details of her past, the more shocking and unnerving Beatrice found these confessions. When it came to the newspaper article about a stabbing and her arrest record, a cocky Estelle pridefully admitted that she was guilty of killing her lover.

"He loved to beat me when he drank too much. No one was there to take care of me but me," she said, adding, "They couldn't prove I did it, so they let me go."

Her crazy eyes suddenly connected with the look of shock on Beatrice's face. Bea recognized the relationship between Estelle's moral decline and her self-preservation. As a small child, she had climbed a mountain of loss and pain, growing up totally alone, absent any loving guidance. First overwhelmed by grief at the loss of the two people she loved, then betrayed by a greedy aunt who abandoned her into poverty, she was forced into child labor and abused by a nun and then thrown out into the street by that woman's greed. Sister Agnes, who bore responsibility for Estelle's spiritual and physical nurturing, instead became a deliberate contributor to Estelle's trauma.

An epiphany of precipitous force hit Beatrice like a bolt of lightning. She could clearly see the string of events that led to the creation of this soulless creature, increasingly consumed by the need to survive and infused with bitterness and hatred as she aged.

Estelle was the actual whore, and Bea, the innocent proxy forced to receive accusatory punishment as Estelle tried to relieve her own madness of guilt. Her aunt's betrayal of her at such a young age made it impossible for her to trust anyone and created in her a consistent, accusatory mindset that someone was trying to steal what was hers. She made Bea her proxy inner child and forced her to shoplift in a dysfunctional attempt to restore the possessions she had been helpless to prevent being stolen from her. The resulting anger and hatred fueled Estelle's bruising of Bea's body.

All these revelations ignited Bea's understanding of what powered Estelle's substance of being. It was hardly surprising when she attacked Bea one last time. Estelle was easily disarmed, but the attack shook Beatrice to her core. The disconnect in Estelle's eyes temporarily vanished into a connection with insanity as she brandished a knife she had taken from Bea's kitchen drawer. As Estelle waved the knife in her face, childhood memories of Estelle waving knives above her tiny fingers and threatening to cut them off flashed through Bea's mind.

Estelle's admission that she had killed a man added to Bea's freshly revived memories of the woman's past threats to her fingers, prompting her to call 9-1-1 without hesitation and have Estelle hospitalized.

Beatrice was done. She had given all she had the strength to give. She told the doctor she could not be responsible for Estelle's care any longer as she feared for her safety. The results of Estelle's MRI and blood work revealed what would have been a shocking diagnosis had it not been for the fresh revelation of Estelle's past: neurosyphilis, untreated tertiary syphilis dormant for over forty years, possibly longer; deteriorating cerebral tissue interrupting brain function, causing her mania and continued psychosis and mental decline, also possibly responsible for a multitude of internal injuries to her vascular system.

Beatrice sat down, paralyzed, processing the diagnosis that solidified and deepened her understanding of the intricate woven fabric of Estelle's life and madness. As she began processing Estelle's diagnosis, she suddenly felt lightheaded, and her heart began to race. It suddenly occurred to her that Estelle's infection might have been transmitted to Bea herself through Rod's abuse. Terror gripped her, and her hands began to tremble. Unable to hold back her tears, she looked up at the doctor and asked if she was at risk. After explaining to him why she had concerns and needed answers, she was grateful for his compassion as he assured her that the disease had likely been in a dormant state for the last thirty to forty years.

He agreed to Bea's request for a blood test to confirm a negative diagnosis. It would take three days to obtain the results—three days of anxiety and depression before she would have an answer. Nightmares dominated her sleep. One of Rod's cold, dead hands of rotting flesh reached out to touch her from his grave. His whispers of hatred, his maniacal laughter, and gloating retribution for her having exposed his abuse finally jolted her awake, soaked with sweat.

Her apprehension caused terrible memories to surface and spread; despondence brought her to the brink of wanting to end her pain in the blackness of nonexistence. She lay in bed weeping; her tears flowed from a place of deep emptiness. She felt drained of every vestige of the confidence she had managed to muster that she could overcome the past. Voices in her head screamed to let go. The journey wasn't worth the struggle—memories of Rod's torment aligned with the terrifying possibility that he had infected her.

On the third day, her phone rang, and a woman's condescending voice said, "Your sexually transmitted disease test result was confirmed negative. Call your doctor with any questions." Bea's cheeks burned at the perceived judgment in the woman's tone of voice as the call ended abruptly with a click, followed by the finality of a dial tone.

Relief flooded Beatrice. Suddenly, she was embarrassed that she had willingly picked up hot coals of melodramatic assumptions and danced to her own frantic music on a stage set with props painted in the intense colors of her past misery. Then, feelings of compassion and mercy overwhelmed her. Estelle's condition was terminal; she was placed in a nursing facility until hospice became necessary. Bea could be at peace with her decision and her efforts to assist Estelle in the final years of her life.

Her last visit with Estelle shortly before her death left Beatrice with an everlastingly horrifying image. An inexperienced caregiver was attempting to feed Estelle strawberry Jell-O, unaware of her inability to swallow. The result was a haunting scene of a pale gray face, a dead look of disconnected eyes, and what appeared to be blood running down both corners of her mouth and dripping onto the front of her hospital gown. The stain resembled a blood-soaked chest wound.

The shocking scene triggered a panic attack in Bea. Letting go of the privacy curtain she was clutching to steady herself, she rushed out of the building to the parking lot and into the safety and seclusion of her car. Fighting to breathe and steady her trembling hands, she suddenly remembered the voice of her therapist and applied techniques she had learned to help stabilize her body and mind.

Although Estelle and Beatrice were united by their parallel grief of childhood losses and abuse, what separated them was Estelle's final transformation from innocence to bitterness, her surrender at a time in history when gender oppression was all but inescapable, her transformation from Estelle, emotionally wounded, to Estelle, tragically sinking into immorality and madness.

Bea's resentment, anger, and bitterness gradually dissolved into peaceful forgiveness. Forgiveness had its price, though letting go of resentment. She still had to live with the consequences of the emotional and physical trauma she had suffered: enduring lifelong recurring pain from spinal injuries, struggling with social anxiety, constant awkwardness, avoiding relationships out of fear of rejection, feeling a complete lack of self-worth, and at times fearing that God Himself would not see her as worthy of love.

When the time came, Beatrice arranged a funeral for Estelle and paid for it herself, even though she would be the only person there. To show respect for the finality of Estelle's tragic existence, Bea planned the affair in carefully thought-out detail. Draped across the crest of Estelle's casket lay a large spray of red gardenias to symbolize forgiveness and understanding. The bouquet was tied with a white satin ribbon, representing innocence, embroidered with a brilliant crimson thread down its center in recognition of all the trials Estelle had endured in her youth.

She said a silent prayer for her foster mother's eternal peace and hoped that all those responsible for harming her would receive a fitting spiritual punishment. Beatrice regretted that she felt no loss or sadness at Estelle's passing—only relief that she would no longer be responsible for Estelle's care. At the graveside, she watched as the casket was gently lowered into the ground, satisfied with the follow-through and execution of Estelle's burial. Before turning to leave, Bea consciously stood tall, with shoulders back and head up. Her eyes connected with the intensity of life buzzing all around her.

This closure helped bring understanding and acceptance of how her past impacted her journey toward future purpose. Rejecting the character pollution of self-pity, she accepted the reality that the crimson threads of Estelle's tragic life were irrevocably woven through the tapestry of her own existence.

Beatrice acknowledged that Estelle was responsible for her insecurities and her inability to trust. The walls and boundaries she constructed as a child living in constant fear had become barriers, making her decline invitations because of painful discomfort born of social anxiety, avoid close relationships that might end in abandonment, or shy away from open doors of opportunity that she might otherwise have been able to take advantage of. She still suffered from the constant oppression, the continuous monitoring, the shame and degradation beaten into her by Estelle and Rod.

She knew she would spend a lifetime struggling to compost memories of the many transgressions against herself and Andy, turning them into fertilizer for a productive future, but she vowed to reconstruct herself in a way that allowed her to value all that she had survived. By pure force of will, she was determined to prove deserving of life despite the gaping rents in the fabric of her identity.

At this moment, Bea felt reborn—the weight of responsibility was lifted from her with every step as she walked back to her car after the interment. Suddenly, she noticed the fresh colors of spring bursting to life as sunlight broke through the clouds, lighting up the beautifully manicured grounds of the cemetery as she opened the door of her treasured eight-year-old El Camino and slid onto the worn vinyl seat. She took a deep breath and exhaled the anxiety of her day.

Reaching for the sunglasses she had left on the dashboard, she adjusted them on the bridge of her nose, turned the key in the ignition, and sat for a moment, listening to the purr of the engine. Then she flicked on the radio and turned up the volume. One of her favorite tunes was playing Journey's Don't Stop Believing. "The timing of this particular song playing on the radio at this particular moment struck her as providential. For her, it was an anthem of perseverance through hardship. She cranked up the volume a little more as she drove along the narrow pavement that would take her out of the cemetery.

Chapter

11

Andy

My sister's name was Beatrice. She was the one and only positive figure in my childhood, the one and only source of connection to emotional sanctuaries of temporary peace. I remember her rocking me, the coolness of her hands as she wiped away the blood dripping from my wounds with bits of her clothing, washed the tiny open blisters on my hands, and caressed my head when I laid it on her small frame as tears ran down my face.

Hers was the love that soothed my pain, the mother spirit that lifted me from the ashes of my sorrow and rejection. She alone gave all that she did not receive as a child—protection, acceptance, and empathy for my pain; as she watched the abuse, she was powerless to stop. I saw the fear in her eyes when she faced the immanent obstacle of abuse and its painful consequences, unable to understand the reasons why.

Our relationship was the only treasure I possessed. Sadly, it was formed by the cruelty of our oppressors and our mutual determination to survive. I have no memories of how I became a part of that asylum of dysfunction. My memories start with words spoken in anger as I sat, confused, my thumb in my mouth, anchored there by the suction of anxiety to the point of pain.

Bea is the only one I can remember who changed my clothes and washed my face. My thick, wiry hair had a mind of its own, but she tried to run a comb through it anyway. She set bowls of cereal in front of me when I was hungry. As we got older, the screams of our tormentors grew louder and more intense and were accompanied by anger and physical pain. We were no more than tiny gardeners with limited tools to dig and weed, pull and push, and maintain everything for Estelle, whose expectations of an impeccably groomed landscape were impossible for two small children to meet.

Education came last after all of Estelle's daily "quotas" were met. I watched as Beatrice was forced to use a scythe almost equal to her height. She would swing its curved blade back and forth, slicing through the tall wheat grass. Then we would make it into a pile and feed it to Estelle's pathetic attempt at farming livestock using Bea and me as her inexperienced farm hands. She tromped out to the field to ridicule us or demand that we redo what she felt was not done to her standards. If she was dissatisfied, she denied us water or refused to let us enter the house, even to pee.

We were her unpaid lackeys—only there to serve. I was called "nigger lips" or "cock sucker," but most often just plain "nigger." I came from the same Korean orphanage as my sister, but I am half African American and half Korean. I was left at the door of Harry Holt's orphanage by my Black father, whose only legacy was an attached letter that explained his son's abandonment: my mother did not want me. She could not survive being ostracized and rejected by her family. About to be shipped out to another battle location, my father was desperate to keep me safe. He felt the orphanage, with its manifesto of Harry Holt's well-known intentions of acquiring homes and families in the United States for outcast mixed-race babies, was his only safe option.

When I was around eight years old, I remember overhearing a conversation about my father contacting the adoption society, trying to find me. Unfortunately, because my father suffered from what used to be called a mental disorder or shell shock (what we now know as PTSD), he was unable to gain the stability needed to legally obtain custody of me. Soon afterward, he took his own life.

I did not understand the full force of this tragedy until I was much older, at a time in my life when the knowledge added a mountain of grief and regret. My being biracial opened a door of bigoted hatred that, for Estelle, never closed. My first introduction to her husband, Rod, her sidekick of deplorable cruelty, was terrifying. He was tall with a ruddy, pockmarked complexion. He had huge hands. One hand could wrap around my neck with ease and lift me up off the floor so that he could stare into my eyes while my face turned red from lack of oxygen. He had dark, angry eyes and a perpetual sneer of anger. My fear of him was constant.

Estelle would decide on a crime and beat us into an admission of guilt, even though we were innocent. She would almost drown my sister in the kitchen sink for the same reason, then play relay when Rod came home to finish the punishment after a forced admission of guilt.

His sadistic delight in delivering punishment was emotionally apocalyptic for both of us. I watched as he unscrewed the light bulb out of one of the lamps and repeatedly shoved Bea's fingers into the socket, making her body jolt. Her screams and terrified tears excited him.

He used the buckle end of belts on our backs, bottoms, and legs. Rod's hatred of us was expressed not only in physical abuse but sexual abuse as well. Once, he demanded that Bea molest me while he watched. She defiantly refused, telling him No! the only time I ever heard her say the word No Rod's eyes burned with sadistic, uncontrolled rage, and he screamed through gritted teeth, "I will get even with you, you piece of shit!" He beat her in front of me until she could not stand after he slammed her head into a wall.

Soon after, on a sunny afternoon, he arrived home unexpectedly and grabbed me, dragging me to a secluded spot and forcibly impaling my body in the ultimate act of degradation and shame, an act of vicious retaliation. Afterward, he told me to find my sister and show her what her big mouth had done. His cruel act broke both of us into unrepairable pieces. I don't think she ever recovered from feeling responsible for what happened to me.

Her refusal to participate in violating me was existential loyalty to me, as she knew and willingly accepted that a beating would surely follow as the consequence of refusing his demand. Later, she must have regretted with every fiber of her being that she had underestimated Rod's capacity for grotesque retribution. Her sudden disappearance not long afterward had an even worse impact on me.

They said she ran off and got married, got married to who? Being cut off from communication with her was unbearable. I felt lost and angry. There was nowhere to channel my emotions. Estelle now directed toward me everything that prodded her insane fantasies. Rod's continued sexual abuse impacted my sanity. Estelle's accusations of my sexual misconduct reached the hideous extent of her duct-taping boxing gloves onto my hands.

Their insane, demonic oppression was gradually sucking me into the dark hole of their depravity. One night, Estelle started slamming me with a piece of rubber hose while screaming profanities at me. She accused me of doing exactly what Rod did to me. Beatrice was gone, and I was totally alone in this darkness. Estelle turned into a rabid animal, growling profanities and endlessly slamming my body with the rubber hose while yanking my hair and scratching my face.

The darkness of surrender for the sake of survival was suddenly replaced by the blackness of uncontrolled anger when the blackness left the beast lay bleeding on the ground. The sound of sirens penetrated my awareness. Seeing Bea at the police station was like finding the other half of my soul. I embraced her tightly, not wanting to let her go, and drenched her with my tears.

She was my truth; she was my strength to overcome shame, to secure my freedom from Estelle and Rod, to release me to a new life. I now have a new life, but it is polluted by trauma and shame. The memories still haunt me if I let them. My trauma is just that—mine. It belongs to no one else but me. I possess power over me, my life, and my recovery. I choose to move forward as a survivor. Moving forward requires closing the door to the past, along with all the windows with — complete closure, even if it means leaving my relationship with my sister.

She will never stop loving me because she knows I will not stop loving her. She exists in the closet of my closure, still relevant, still a part of who I am. Her goodness and caring nurtured me through the darkest parts of my life and helped me hold onto my goodness and the confidence that my life is worth living in the future that awaits me. I know the strength my sister possesses and the life she deserves, and she deserves it without the daily reminder of her past that is reflected in my eyes, in the guilt she places on herself for her imagined failure.

I spoke repeatedly of my gratitude for all she meant to me before I departed from her life. Now, she must find closure from her own trauma, which belongs to her and only her. My sister will find her wings and fly. One day, we will meet with smiles of recognition as our eyes connect with love and understanding.

Chapter

12

Breaking Free

The deeper sorrow carves into your being, the more joy you can contain." This line from a poem by Khalil Gibran struck a chord of connection the instant Beatrice read it. In sharing her story, she chose to carve open her soul, exposing the wounds of the heart and the humiliation of the body, to encourage others to scale walls built by trauma, tragedy, and loss, land on both feet on the other side; and start a journey toward healing. There is a joy to be found in the completed journey.

A journey requires packing bags with the things we need for grooming and comfort. Packing for emotional journeys is different. Our bags are weighed down with memories, regrets, sadness, self-loathing, shame, fear, and resentment. We drag these painful burdens toward the future, unpacking relics of the past at each destination, laying them out for display, and reviewing them each day. Seeing ourselves as unworthy of love, we often sabotage possibilities for future happiness, willingly laying down our hopes and dreams in a forest of invisibility, unaware that we are armed for liberation, needing only courage to pull the trigger.

Breaking free requires cutting the threads that bind us to the past. The most powerful scissors are simply kindness to ourselves and forgiveness of those responsible for the events that contributed to a shattered self-image—cutting away the loathing and blame aimed at the ones who caused our transformation into wounded beings.

Years of struggle and therapy helped Beatrice slice through the past and let go of the one person she loved—her brother. Releasing ties to the past also meant releasing the monstrous grief she felt over her perceived failure to protect him and coming to understand and believe that her love for him was integral to whatever goodness of character he had managed to hold onto.

There were times when echoes of the past, written on her body, reached out to lay claim to confidence, murmuring that her existence on Earth was a mistake, underserved. Such was the case each day with her morning grooming routine, which included camouflaging bald spots where hair once grew before it had been ripped from her scalp along with tiny pieces of bleeding flesh. She was running fingers over the raised texture of scars when bathing could spark recollections of the scenarios that gave them birth, every touch pressing a rewind and replay button in her mind and causing the vicious words that accompanied them to reverberate in her ears.

Scars that run deeper than flesh are the ones hardest to overcome. Although she tried numerous times to learn how to swim, her determination was undermined when she found herself unable to conquer the panic that overwhelmed her senses at the pool when water came close to her nostrils.

Above all, breaking free requires sifting through shades of gray to find the colors of joy, staying faithful to the task at hand, and not succumbing to the bondage of self-pity and grief. Sitting on her covered porch while looking out at the bay, watching the constant in and out of the waves, the rise and fall of the tides around this peaceful little island in the Pacific Northwest—her home for over thirty years—she finds herself profoundly grateful that this was the destination of her life's journey. She is loved by two beautiful daughters and by the man she created them with—the captain of a Bering Sea crabber and, in later years, captain of a southeast Alaska gillnetter. He is a cultured man, kind, gentle, understanding, and accepting of her self-perceived imperfections.

Born of Norwegian stock—a heritage she embraced with pride—he comfortably filled the holes of her missing identity, giving a gift of ethnicity for her daughters, with all its features of cultural celebration and holiday rituals. She embraced it all wholeheartedly: boiling potatoes prior to rolling them into balls for lefse; cooking lutefisk to a jellied consistency of perfection; baking the special Scandinavian cookies, pies, and cakes; and hijacking for her own the Scandinavian exclamation, "Uff-dah."

By achieving closure on the past, she was able to propel herself into a future filled with the richness of adventure, love, and purpose, able to create moments of joy that smoothed leathery old memories of sadness. She experienced traveling Alaska's Inside Passage on her husband's fishing vessel, exalting in the salty wind whipping at her hair as the diesel engine vibrated beneath her feet, humming its monotonous song alongside a school of Dall's porpoises that glided playfully near the hull. They leaped sporadically in and out of the foaming wakes as the ship sliced through the sea, surging toward its destination.

There were pods of orca whales; seagulls by the dozen squawking excitedly when they spotted food on the seabed; eagles gliding with massive wings spread wide against a flawless backdrop of deep blue sky, suddenly swooping downward with eyes focused on prey, their sharp, golden talons extended. Beatrice will cherish those breathtakingly beautiful memories of Alaska for the rest of her life.

They and other experiences gave birth to smiles, especially the experience of motherhood—soft, tiny hands intertwined in her fingers, memories of the purest love an innocent child offers—countering and cleansing the pollution of remembered rejections.

These days, in a morning ritual of pleasant anticipation, Bea clutches her mug of steaming coffee and inhales the pleasant aroma while savoring its satisfying flavor. Sharing her morning coffee with the sun as it pokes its golden rods of light through the clouds or with the friendly, gently tapping rain on the roof, she looks across the bay to familiar sounds of squealing seagulls as they glide across the endless sky. After finally vanquishing the chaos that ruled her life for decades, she is filled with gratitude for the happiness and fulfillment she has been able to experience.

Healing has taken many years of effort, continually striving to fit the broken pieces of herself together, not knowing what the original template was supposed to look like. The emotional journey continues. Because of empty holes waiting to be filled with pieces that don't exist, she may always feel somewhat incomplete, her joy covered with a thin layer of sadness like mist interrupting the clarity of sunlight.

In 2014, after social media had become popular and ubiquitous, Beatrice decided to type her brother's name into an internet search in the hope of obtaining a discreet glimpse at his life, only to find that he had died four years earlier. A resurgence of grief washed over her as she sat frozen in front of her computer screen. Her only consolation lay in a pair of photos posted by his family—a portrait of him with a beautiful smile revealing white teeth, a wife and grown daughter and son, their arms intertwined lovingly around his neck, embracing him. His eyes were filled with joy as he looked into the camera lens, connected with Bea's, brimming with tears.

As she read his family's words of grief and love from the years-old post that announced Andy's death, her tears ran in a trail down her cheeks, and memories resurfaced. She believed that if his family had known of her existence, they would have found a way to contact her, and she accepted her exclusion from her brother's life with understanding. Having for decades held his humiliating secrets in a padlocked iron urn of loyalty; she drew comfort from the fact that this act of love would be her and Andy's one enduring connection.

She felt his metaphysical presence as she wept and traced a finger over the image of his smiling face, framed by unruly hair peppered with gray. A whisper escaped her lips, ignited by the grief erupting from her heart, "I regret we did not have the opportunity to share our collective victories and joys, Andy."

After the initial shock of his passing settled into a reality of loss and sadness, gratitude washed over her in the realization that the sacrifice of his presence in her life had granted each of them the freedom to reconstruct their identity, heal many wounds, and embrace a love of self.

She stared into the smiling eyes in the photo and felt that familiar misty sadness, now mingling with the peaceful contentment of discovery. A soft whisper escaped her lips, "Your smile, little brother, gifts my soul with peace. You will forever continue to be a part of me."

I am grateful to my editor, Christina Dubois, who helped make this book possible.